which?
essential guid

M
CIVIL CLAIM

D0234235

❝ Even if you have lawyers dealing with your claim for you, it can sometimes seem as if you have entered an Alice in Wonderland world where everyone knows the rules of the game except you. ❞

Melanie McDonald

About the author

Melanie McDonald has been in practice at the Bar at No 5 Chambers in Birmingham since 1991. Her practice is exclusively civil common law including personal injury and clinical negligence, as well as education, community care and mental health. She appears regularly in the County Court and has also dealt with a number of High Court and Court of Appeal cases. She is married with three children and divides her time between the Welsh borders and Spain.

essential guides

MAKING A
CIVIL CLAIM

MELANIE McDONALD

For Paul Bleasdale QC, who showed me how a straightforward and
practical approach to the law always works best

Which? Books are commissioned and published by Which? Ltd,
2 Marylebone Road, London NW1 4DF
Head of Which? Books: Angela Newton
Project management for Which? Books: Luke Block
Email: books@which.co.uk

Distributed by Littlehampton Book Services Ltd, Faraday Close, Durrington, Worthing,
West Sussex BN13 3RB

British Library Cataloguing in Publication Data
A catalogue record for this book is available from the British Library

Copyright © Which? Ltd 2007

ISBN 978 1 84490 037 4

Author's acknowledgements
I'm particularly grateful to District Judge Jane Ingram and Anne Smith of Harrisons'
solicitors in Welshpool for their sensible comments and suggestions based on their
own extensive experience of dealing with civil claims. Also to my colleagues at No 5
Chambers in Birmingham for their input; to my clerks, in particular Martin Hulbert and
Abdul Hafeez, and to Tony McDaid, the Senior Practice Manager, for his enthusiasm and
support for the project. Thanks also to Chelsey Fox for pointing me in the right direction
in the first place and to Angela Newton and Luke Block of Which? and Emma Callery
who edited the book – all of whom were a delight to work with. Thanks also to Peter
McCarthy at Which? for his comments on the manuscript.

Edited by: Emma Callery
Designed by: Bob Vickers
Index by: Lynda Swindells
Cover photographs by: Alamy
Printed and bound by Scotprint, Scotland

For a full list of Which? Books, please call 01903 828557, access our website at
www.which.co.uk, or write to Littlehampton Book Services.
For other enquiries call 0800 252 100.

Contents

Introduction

Civil claims are cases involving private disputes between individuals, companies and/or public authorities. When a crime is committed, the state, through the police and the Crown Prosecution Service, steps in to ensure, as far as possible, that justice is done.

But what if your problem has been caused by actions that are not necessarily against the criminal law, but which nevertheless have caused you financial loss, physical or mental injury or emotional upset? This is where the civil courts come in.

This book is intended to provide a practical guide to using the civil justice system in England and Wales. The information it contains should enable you to:

- Become familiar with how the civil courts operate.
- Understand the jargon.
- Decide whether you want to go to court at all or whether you should try to sort out the dispute in some other way.
- Understand the financial implications of a civil claim.
- Know where to go for further information.

Over the last ten years, there have been a number of important changes in how the civil courts operate in this country. The introduction of conditional fees has meant that many people who previously couldn't afford to take a claim through the courts can now do so. At the same time, the introduction of new rules governing court

procedure has attempted to deal with the problems of exorbitant legal costs and lengthy delays, which used to give the courts such a bad name. This is not to say that either conditional fees or the new rules have been entirely successful in creating a user-friendly system, but it is certainly much easier than it used to be to make (or defend) a civil claim.

Nobody wants to go to court, but sometimes a situation or problem develops that simply cannot be ignored or resolved in any other way. Most people will have lawyers to advise them on the legal aspects of their case and whether they have a good chance of winning; but even with their help and advice there will almost certainly be times when the process is stressful and frustrating. An understanding of how the system works should help you to remain in control and able to take the decisions that are right for your situation. At the end of the day, it is your case and you will have the final say about what happens.

LITIGANT IN PERSON

If you're thinking of going it alone, as a litigant in person, you will be taking responsibility for preparing and presenting your case in accordance with a complex set of rules and procedures. This can be very daunting, especially if you're facing an opponent who is legally represented. It will take time and energy, but you should never be afraid to ask for help and information about what needs to be done. Court staff, judges and even your opponent's lawyers are usually very willing to explain court procedure and any requirements that you need to comply with.

In any event, whether or not you have the benefit of legal representation, it will help to know as much as possible about how the civil courts work and what to expect if you should happen to find yourself involved in or on the brink of formal court proceedings. This book explains the process of getting a civil case to trial and also the possibilities that exist for settling a claim before the case ever gets that far.

WHAT ARE CIVIL CLAIMS?

Although we usually think of courts as places where criminal trials take place, the civil courts also deal with an enormous range of cases: disagreements between neighbours, people who've been injured in an accident at work or on the road, faulty goods; the kind of things that go wrong in everyday life and sometimes cannot be sorted out without outside help. The ultimate way of sorting things out in the civil courts is to have a trial, when the evidence and arguments are heard by a judge, who then decides all the matters in dispute and gives judgment for one side or the other.

A comparison of cases heard in criminal and civil courts

Criminal	Civil
Cases are investigated by the police and are almost always brought to court by the Crown Prosecution Service (CPS)	The decision to take a case to court is made by one or other of the individuals concerned in a dispute
Most cases are heard in the Magistrates Court or the Crown Court	Most cases are heard in the County Court
In the Crown Court, a jury decides the case and the judge deals with the law and sentencing	In the County Court, the case is usually heard by a single judge who decides whether the defendant is at fault and what should be done to put matters right. (The exceptions to the rule are actions against the police and defamation)
The case has to be proved beyond reasonable doubt - so that the magistrates or jury are sure of their decision	The case is proved on the balance of probabilities - that is, using the test of what is more likely than not
The purpose of a criminal trial is to establish whether the defendant is guilty and, if so, punish him	The purpose of a civil trial is to find out whether the defendant is liable, and, if so, order that the injured party should be recompensed

Reasons why you might want to pursue a claim in the civil court

- I've suffered an injury as a result of an accident at work.
- I've fallen out with my business partner and now she's changed the locks of our shop and refuses to let me have access to the accounting books.
- My landlord refuses to carry out repairs to our house even though there is black mould all over the kitchen and bathroom and my children keep getting ill.
- My neighbours are really noisy and ignore my requests not to play loud music late at night and in the early morning.
- The car dealer told me that I was getting a good deal but I've now discovered the car he sold me was written off in an accident and should never have been back on the road.
- The surveyor who did the valuation for our mortgage failed to spot a major structural problem and now we've been told the house is virtually unsaleable.
- I'm a wheelchair user and I recently went on a singles holiday. I couldn't get access to any of the leisure facilities and the attitude of the staff to me was awful. I think I might have a claim for discrimination.

Reasons why you might be on the receiving end of a claim

- I was involved in a road accident, but I'm sure it wasn't my fault.
- We had a party at my house and someone managed to open the door to the cellar and fall down the stairs while they were drunk. Now they're claiming damages.
- I've got a dispute with my neighbour about our boundary. I put up a fence along where I think the boundary is but now he has issued proceedings against me.
- My husband died last year and as if that wasn't enough to deal with, it seems he had a mistress who is claiming she is entitled to some kind of payment.
- Our builder did such a bad job that I refused to pay him until he sorted it out, now he's suing me for the money.
- I haven't been able to keep up with my mortgage payments and now the bank wants to repossess the house.
- I've just split up from my boyfriend. We lived together for five years. It was my house and he never contributed to the mortgage, but now he's saying that just because he put in new windows and landscaped the garden he's entitled to a share in it.

Preliminaries

This section is designed to give a few pointers as to how the civil claims system works and what you may need to think about before taking things further. While it is not intended to cover everything, many of the topics touched upon here are considered in more detail later on.

1

Before you go further

If you are seriously having to contemplate the possibility of going to court to resolve a civil dispute, there are a number of things you will need to consider. This section will help get you off on the right foot.

HOW CAN I BE SURE OF WINNING MY CASE?

The short answer is you can't. It is almost impossible to predict the outcome of a civil claim. Your lawyers may advise you that you have a good chance of success or you may read in the paper of cases where people who seem to have been in exactly the same position as you have emerged triumphant from the rough and tumble of the courtroom; but each set of circumstances giving rise to a civil claim is entirely unique to the people involved, and this means that you can never be sure what is going to happen at trial. So, until your opponent makes you an offer you can't refuse, or the case is finally determined in your favour, you will have to learn to live with an element of risk.

However, the uncertainty about the outcome applies equally to your opponent. They also have to assess the risks and may well decide that it is better to compromise than risk the costs and loss of face of a defeat at trial. This is why so many claims settle before the case gets to a final hearing.

Out-of-court settlements

One of the advantages of an out-of-court settlement is that you can be more creative and flexible in the terms of the agreement that you reach. The court has a range of powers that it can use to try to put things right for the injured party, but there are limits on what it can do.

WHAT DO I REALLY WANT TO ACHIEVE?

This is an important question and one that you need to think about right at the beginning. The answer may help you decide whether going to court will provide the solution you need, or whether there may be other ways of sorting out the problem, which might work better for you. If there is more than one answer, try to place them in order of importance. Here are some possibilities:

- I want full financial compensation.
- I want to find out exactly what happened.

 For more information on out-of-court settlements, see page 24 for settlement as a result of mediation and the whole subject of settlement is covered on pages 105–18.

- I want someone to apologise to me for what went wrong.
- I want to find a way of putting things right with my neighbour.
- I want to make sure that nobody has to go through what I did.
- I want the full protection of a court order.
- I want someone to look at all the evidence and decide who was at fault.

You may also find it helpful to carry out the exercise in reverse, identifying the things that are not so important to you. For example, does it really matter that your former boss apologises if you're never going to have to see him again? Would you be willing to forego your opponent paying your costs if the matter can be sorted out quickly?

MAKING AMENDS

Although the court has a range of remedies that it can use to try to put things right, there are limits to its powers and you may find that the solution you are looking for isn't necessarily available through the courts.

What the court can do

- **Order a person or company to pay damages,** financial compensation, either to reimburse financial loss or expenditure, or to compensate for physical or mental injury or (in certain circumstances) upset feelings.
- **Grant an injunction** Make an order that forbids the defendant from doing a specified act, such as threatening the claimant (a negative injunction).

Or
Make an order that the defendant should take some specified action to put matters right, such as take down a fence wrongly erected on a neighbour's land (a positive injunction).

- **Make a declaration** A formal statement clarifying the law or facts in respect of a specific situation, such as the exact position of a boundary, or whether medical treatment can be lawfully given to someone who has refused it.
- **Order an account or enquiries** in a case where there might have been financial mismanagement.
- **Make a freezing order** Freezing assets such as bank accounts and property dealings, where there is a risk of the money being moved to avoid a judgment.

What the court can't do

- It cannot punish people or penalise companies for misconduct (except in certain specified cases, such as unlawful eviction, where it can order 'exemplary damages').
- It cannot insist that people behave well. It cannot order someone to apologise for behaving badly or take back hurtful or insulting words (though it can find that the words were untrue).
- However serious an injury, the court cannot order compensation if it finds that the injury was caused accidentally and no one was at fault.
- The court cannot make someone pay damages or costs if they don't have the money.

11

COSTS: THE HEALTH WARNING

In considering whether or not you want to take the risk and pursue or defend a civil claim, the most important thing you will need to take into account is the financial cost of losing the case. Unless your claim is heard in the small claims court, if you lose, the court will almost certainly order you to pay the winning party's legal costs.

It is not unusual for those costs to be as much as, if not more than, the value of the claim itself. In real terms, that means that you may find yourself having to pay upwards of £5,000 in addition to your own lawyer's bill. On a multi track claim (see page 101), you are probably looking at a minimum of £20,000 and the sky's the limit. It is hardly surprising, then, that managing a civil claim is often as much about dealing with the risk of losing the case as it is about winning.

For most people, the risk can be reduced or eliminated by taking out insurance – either before or after the event that led to the claim (see page 48). If you don't have insurance or any other protection (perhaps from a trade union or because you are getting legal aid), you will need to be very certain indeed that you are going to win your case. The fact that you are a litigant in person or that your lawyer did not present the case as you wanted, or that the judge expressed sympathy for your position, will not stop the court from ordering you to pay your opponent's costs if you lose.

❝ A key question for any case is what the cost of losing it would be. ❞

TIME LIMITS

Before you go any further you need to check that you have not missed the deadline for bringing your claim. Different types of claim have different deadlines (see table, opposite).

How long will it all take?

It is always difficult to predict. A straightforward small claims or fast track case (see page 18) should be ready for final hearing between four months and a year after the case has been started in the court. A more complicated case with experts involved will take longer. Most cases should get to trial within two years of the claim being started. The courts are very keen on making sure that unnecessary delay is avoided and if at any stage your opponent seems to be dragging his or her feet, you can always ask the court to move things on.

 Don't forget that a costs order can be enforced against any assets that you have, including your house, your savings or anything else that you own that has a cash value.

Limitation periods

Different types of claim have different deadlines for bringing the claim.

Type of claim	Deadline	Exceptions
Judicial review (challenging a decision made by a public authority)	Three months from when the decision you want to challenge was made/communicated to you	The court may allow extra time if you have a good reason for not complying with the deadline
Defamation – libel (written) and slander (spoken)	One year from the date the words were spoken or published	If there is a good reason for missing the deadline, the court *may* extend the time allowed
Injury on board a ship or aeroplane	Two years from the date of the injury	
Harassment	Six years either from the time the harassment stopped or from the date you found out the identity of the person responsible	
Most personal injury claims (including medical negligence)	Three years from the date of the injury or from the date when you first suspected you might have a claim	If there are very good reasons for the delay and the defendant will not be in a worse position than if the claim was in time, the court *may* allow it to proceed
Contractual and consumer disputes	Six years from the date the agreement was breached	
Professional negligence (e.g. surveyors, financial advisers, solicitors, architects, accountants, etc.)	Six years from the date that the loss was suffered (for example, the day on which a house was purchased as the result of a negligent survey)	If the problem could not have been detected at the time, three years from the date when it could and should have been discovered
Claims to recover land (including money owing under a mortgage)	12 years from the date that the claimant was entitled to possession or the right of possession was interfered with	

Note: Time only starts to run for children when they reach their 18th birthday. So, for example, a child injured in an accident will have until their 21st birthday to bring a personal injury claim.

Overview of the civil courts

Civil claims are processed either in the County Court or the High Court depending on how complicated the case is. Whichever court deals with the claim, the rules and procedures to be followed are the same.

What does the court decide?

The facts	What happened?
The law	How does the law apply to the facts in this particular case?
Liability	Is anyone at fault? If so, who? (Sometimes liability can be split between two or more defendants)
The remedy	What needs to be done to put things right. The idea is that the injured party should be put back into the position they were in before the wrongdoing occurred
Costs	Who is to pay the costs of the legal proceedings?

THE COUNTY COURT

The vast majority of civil claims are dealt with by the County Court. Most towns in England and Wales have their own County Court, usually tucked away inside the Crown Court building, where criminal trials are held, or housed in an anonymous office block near the town centre. They are workaday places consisting of a waiting area, conference rooms where you can talk in private, a series of district judge's offices, where interim applications and small claims are heard, and the more formal court rooms where trials take place. There is also a court office where you go to start a claim or make an application or if you have any queries about how the claim is progressing.

THE HIGH COURT

If your case is particularly complicated, perhaps because it involves an important legal argument or a very large sum of money, it may go to the High Court where a more senior judge will deal with it. The High Court includes a number of specialist courts where the judges have a particular expertise in that area of law (see table, opposite).

There is no hard and fast rule about which cases should be heard in the High Court. Generally speaking, High Court litigation tends to be more expensive.

Ask the expert

How does the judge reach his or her decision?

At trial, the judge hears evidence from witnesses for both sides and then decides what is most likely to have happened. The judge must then decide how the law applies to the particular case with which he or she is concerned. He or she does this first by looking at any laws or regulations that apply and, second, by taking into account previous decisions taken by other courts in similar cases.

If the Court of Appeal or House of Lords has made a ruling that is relevant to your case, the trial judge must follow it. A decision made by a court at the same or lower level can be taken into account by the judge, but he or she is not bound by it.

On the other hand, if the case does raise difficult issues, you or your lawyers may want the case heard by a more senior judge, whose decision is likely to carry more weight. Ultimately, the court itself will decide whether a case is suitable for the High Court.

Specialist courts

If your case falls into a more specialised area of law or commercial activity, it may be dealt with by one of the High Court specialist divisions where the judges have a very high level of expertise in that type of claim (see box, below).

In the High Court

Court	What it covers
Chancery Division	Deals with cases involving wills, property, trusts and other money matters
Commercial Court	Major commercial disputes
Construction and Technology	Complicated building and technical disputes
Administrative Court	Judicial review – where someone wishes to challenge a decision made by a local authority or other public body
Queen's Bench Division	Deals with the vast majority of High Court civil claims, including personal injury, medical negligence and contractual disputes

THE CIVIL PROCEDURE RULES (CPR)

These are the rules that govern civil cases. They apply both to the High Court and the County Court and they cover every aspect of taking a civil claim through the courts. They have to be applied by the court so that they comply with 'the overriding objective' – the principle that all claims should be dealt with as fairly and quickly as possible. In practical terms this means:

- **Cards on the table:** both sides must be open with one another and co-operate with each other as much as possible.
- **Time limits** must be met unless there is a very good reason for not doing so.
- **The court can intervene** at any stage and do whatever it considers necessary to move the case along.
- **Neither party should run up costs** that are out of all proportion to the value of the claim.
- **In addition to the rules,** there are a number of Practice Directions (see box, above left). These set out more detailed requirements about what needs to be done to comply with the rules.

❝ Civil Procedure Rules apply to civil cases in the High Court and County Court. They cover every aspect of making a claim, with the aim of making the process both fair and fast. ❞

CPR – Where to find them in this book

There is a table of the most important rules on pages 202-3. In addition, each section of the book also gives you the particular rules that apply to that part of the procedure if you want to look at them in more detail. The revelevant procedue rules are referred to throughout as **CPR Part XX.**

ON THE RIGHT TRACK

Claims are classified by the court depending on their value. There are three 'tracks' and one of the first things the court does is to decide which track your case should be on.

Small claims track

Claims for damages of less than £5,000 (£1,000 in personal injury and housing disrepair cases) are put on the small claims track. This means that the court expects that the parties will not use lawyers and for that reason, apart from court fees and witness expenses, even if you win, you will not be able to claim any costs. If you think your claim is likely to end up on the small claims track, you will need to think carefully about whether you want to spend money consulting a lawyer when it is unlikely that you will be able to recover the cost. It is probably better in this instance to use one of the free sources of legal advice and information such as the Citizens Advice Bureau. See also the Which? Legal Service information on page 33.

66 Even if you win a small claims case, you are unlikely to be able to reclaim legal costs. **99**

Jargon buster

Action Claim going through the court

Circuit judge County Court judge who deals with fast track and multi track trials, appeals from the district judge and interim applications in more complicated cases

Claimant Person bringing the claim

Costs order Order determining who should pay the legal costs

Damages Financial compensation

Defendant Person against whom the claim is brought

District judge County Court judge who deals with interim applications and small claims and fast track trials

Liability Legal responsibility

Limitation period Time allowed for bringing a claim

Litigant/party Person bringing or defending a claim

Litigation friend Someone bringing a claim either on behalf of a child or an adult who lacks the mental capacity to understand the proceedings

Proceedings Taking a claim through the court

Recorder Lawyer who sits as a part-time judge

Remedy Action ordered by the court to try and make amends

 To find your nearest Citizens Advice Bureau (CAB), see your local phone book or go to www.adviceguide.org.uk.

Fast track

Claims between £5,000 and £15,000 are allocated to the fast track. You will get your legal costs if you win a fast track claim, but the amount your lawyers can claim is subject to strict limits. In most cases this should not affect you, but there may be situations where you are expected to make good any shortfall in your lawyer's fees. You should always find out at the outset what your liability for your own lawyer's costs will be.

Multi track

Claims worth more than £15,000 become multi track claims. The court expects these claims to be more expensive to run and is willing to allow all the costs that it considers were necessary to bring the case to trial or defend it. However, your lawyers will not get costs that the court considers to be unreasonable. All High Court cases are multi track.

MEETING THE TIME LIMITS

Deadlines are set by the court for each stage in the proceedings. The court will not mind if the parties agree minor variations in the timetable; so if you or your opponent need an extra week or two to get witness statements ready or to obtain expert evidence, there's no need to ask the court for permission, although any agreement to vary the time limits must be confirmed in writing. However, if it becomes obvious that the case will not be ready for trial in time for the beginning of the trial window, it will be necessary to make an application to the court. If both sides agree that extra time is needed, the application can be dealt with by the district judge without a hearing.

Usually the court will agree to postpone the trial if there is a good reason to do so, but the parties should not assume that just because they agree, the court's approval will automatically be forthcoming. If only one side wants to postpone the trial, there will usually be a hearing with each party putting their arguments to the district judge. Because the fast track is supposed to be just that, the court can be very reluctant to change the trial date.

> **" The court will usually agree to postpone a trial if there is good reason, but this approval is not given automatically. "**

 To find out more about the different court tracks, go to www.hmcourts-service.gov.uk/infoabout/claims.

Case Study Ms Taylor

Ms Taylor suffered injuries in a road accident. Liability was not disputed by the driver, Mr Brock, but the amount of damages could not be agreed and eventually court proceedings were started. The claim was allocated to the fast track and a trial date was fixed by the court. A few weeks before the trial, Ms Taylor's solicitors decided that she also had a claim for psychiatric problems she had suffered as a result of the accident. They asked the defendant's solicitors to agree to the trial being adjourned and the case being moved to the multi track. The defendant's solicitors refused so an application was made to the court, which decided to hear the application on the day set for the trial.

Ms Taylor's solicitors were so sure they would get the adjournment that they told her she did not need to go to court and her barrister only prepared for the adjournment application. In fact, the judge refused to adjourn the case and insisted that the trial should go ahead. Unsurprisingly, the amount of damages awarded was low, which meant that as the claimant had turned down a previous higher offer, she had to pay some of the defendant's costs. The Court of Appeal rejected her appeal and said that the judge had been right. In a fast track claim, an adjournment is always a last resort and since the lawyers acting for Ms Taylor had not produced evidence to support their argument that she had suffered psychiatric injury, there was no reason for the judge to grant the adjournment.

Taylor v Brock (25 February 2000) Court of Appeal

Case studies

All the case studies in this book are real cases that have been decided by the courts. If you are interested in reading the full written judgment, you will find the High Court and Court of Appeal judgments on the internet.

High Court decisions (EWHC – England and Wales High Court) from 1997 and Court of Appeal decisions (EWCA Civ – England and Wales Court of Appeal Civil) from 1996 can be found on www.bailii.org.uk listed by the year and in alphabetical order.

House of Lords judgments (EWHL – England and Wales House of Lords) from 1996 onwards are posted on www.parliament.the-stationary-office.co.uk. They are also listed by the year and in alphabetical order.

County Court judgments are not usually posted on the internet. The ones in this book can be accessed through www.lawtel.com, which is a specialist legal subscription service.

Alternatives to court

One of the things you must give some thought to right at the outset is whether there may be some other way of dealing with the situation. Various formal and informal ways of resolving disputes are available and you will need to consider whether one of these might be the best way of resolving the dispute.

There are all sorts of reasons for looking at the alternatives to court proceedings. The first and perhaps most important is because there is simply no guarantee that your claim or defence will succeed. Second, although you may decide in the end that court action is the only way forward, the court will expect you at least to have considered alternative ways of reaching an agreement with your opponent. This is known as alternative dispute resolution (or ADR) and includes each of the methods described to the right. Where someone has refused to consider ADR without a good reason, even if they win their case at trial, the judge may decide not to follow the normal rule of making the loser pay all costs of the court proceedings.

There are a number of different sorts of ADR, not all of which will necessarily be suitable for your situation. They include the items listed above right.

- Complaints
- The ombudsman
- Mediation
- Round table meeting
- Arbitration
- Criminal Injuries Compensation Scheme (CICS).

&& The court expects you to at least consider alternative ways of reaching an agreement to avoid going to court. &&

For further information about all types of ADR, go to www.adrnow.gov.uk or www.cls-direct.org.uk.

Useful addresses

There are many ombudsmen internet resources ranging from local government to parliamentary and other bodies. For more information, see Useful addresses on pages 210–12.

You will also find advice about how to use the ombudsmen on the Citizens Advice Bureau website, www.adviceguide.org.uk, and the Advice Service Alliance ADR website at www.adrnow.org.uk.

Case Study   Ms Dunnett

The claimant, Ms Dunnett, kept horses in a field adjoining a railway. Someone left a gate open and three of her horses were killed when they strayed on to the track. She sued Railtrack even though it was impossible to say who had left the gate open and was therefore responsible for the loss of the horses. She lost her case at trial and then appealed to the Court of Appeal. One of the judges at the Court of Appeal strongly recommended that ADR should be considered, even at that late stage. Ms Dunnett was willing to use ADR but Railtrack refused because they were confident they would win the appeal – which indeed they did. However, the Court of Appeal refused to order Ms Dunnett to pay Railtrack's costs of the appeal. It said Railtrack's lawyers should have been willing to consider ADR since it might have been possible to resolve the situation with an apology or an explanation rather than incur the costs of a full hearing in front of the Court of Appeal.

Dunnett v Railtrack (2002) EWCA Civ 302

❝ If someone refuses to consider ADR and wins the case at trial, the judge may not make the loser pay all costs. ❞

To read the full written judgment for this case, go to www.bailii.org.uk where all Court of Appeal decisions are listed by the year and in alphabetical order.

Case Study Frank Cowl

Frank Cowl lived in a residential care home run by Plymouth County Council. When it was announced that the home was to close, Mr Cowl and the other residents challenged the council's decision in the court by making an application for judicial review. The council suggested that instead of going to court, the dispute could be dealt with under the council's own complaints procedure. This would involve an independent panel making a decision that the council did not have to follow but would take into account when making its final decision.

The case ended up in the Court of Appeal. Not only did the residents lose, but they were strongly criticised by the court for failing to give any good reason why they would not agree to the council's suggestion of ADR. The judge said that the use of public money for the court action was indefensible.

Frank Cowl & Others v Plymouth County Council (2001) EWCA Civ 1935

MAKING A COMPLAINT

Many professional organisations, local authorities, hospitals, etc. have their own formal complaints procedure, which they should tell you about at the time you first raise your case with them (if they don't, you can always ask if there is a complaints procedure that you can use). If your dispute is about the quality of service you received from one of these, it is almost always worth using this in the first instance. If you are not satisfied with the outcome, there is nothing to stop you from taking the case any further, either to the ombudsman (see opposite) or to court.

The pros and cons of making a complaint

Pros	Cons
• It's cheap (you won't need a lawyer) and (relatively) quick.	• It may ultimately not be able to provide adequate recompense.
• If your claim is rejected, there's nothing to stop you taking it to the ombudsman or to court.	• You may feel that an internal complaints procedure is weighted against you.

OMBUDSMAN

The ombudsman investigates complaints by members of the public against a number of organisations, government departments and local authorities (see box, below). The ombudsman will only become involved if all the other existing complaints procedures have been exhausted. On receipt of the papers, the ombudsman will investigate the case and produce a report setting out his findings and any action that needs to be taken as a result. Where the complaint relates to the private sector, the ombudsman has the power to order the organisation concerned to pay compensation.

The ombudsmen responsible for investigating local authorities and government departments are limited to deciding whether there has been 'maladministration' that has resulted in an injustice. If there has been

> **"The ombudsman will only become involved if all the other existing complaints procedures have been exhausted."**

maladministration they can make recommendations, including the payment of compensation. These recommendations are not binding but in practice they are almost always accepted by the public authority concerned.

If your main concern is to find out what happened and to have your concerns upheld by an independent body, the ombudsman may provide an effective way of resolving your case.

The pros and cons of using an ombudsman

Pros	Cons
• It's cheap (again no lawyer required).	• It may take a long time for the report to be produced.
• It may provide an acceptable remedy, either by way of compensation or apology or an acknowledgement that your case was badly handled.	• Compensation and other remedies available may be limited and less than you would get by taking the case to court.
	• If your complaint is rejected, your opponent may use the report as evidence against your case in any subsequent court proceedings (although the court will make its own decision on the basis of all the evidence – so this will not, in itself, be enough to lose the case).

MEDIATION

Mediation provides an opportunity for the parties to meet, usually on neutral territory, to see if the dispute can be settled. A mediator is appointed and acts as a go-between in the negotiations. A skilful mediator can enable both sides to find a way of working through their differences and reach an effective agreement. This may involve the payment of money but it can also include much more creative solutions than would be available at court. For example, an apology, a promise that things will be done differently from now on, or a framework enabling the parties to continue to deal with one another in the future (which may be very helpful if the dispute is between neighbours, members of the same family, or business partners). Mediation comes in various shapes, sizes and degrees of formality. Community and court mediation schemes are now widely available. Alternatively, a mediation can be set up by your solicitor if everyone is in agreement that it's worth trying.

Costs

Usually, the cost of a mediation is split between the two sides and it includes the mediator's fee and hiring a suitable venue (you will need at least three rooms: one for each party and a larger room for everyone to meet up in). In addition, it is usual for both sides to take their lawyers, sometimes both barrister and solicitor, to the mediation, which further adds to the cost.

Unlike court proceedings, there will be no winning side, so unless there is specific provision for costs to be paid under the terms of any agreement, you will not be able to recover the mediation costs, although if you are receiving legal aid or your claim is supported by an insurance company or trade union, they

---

Mediation costs

The National Mediation Helpline (see box at the foot of page 26) provides a scale of charges for using one of their accredited mediators (all prices include VAT):

Small claims track: £58.50 an hour for each side

Fast track: £98.70 an hour for each side

Multi track (up to £50,000): £109.86 an hour for each side

Multi track (£50,000 +): To be agreed with the mediator

The helpline suggests that a small claims mediation might take an hour and a fast track case three hours to mediate. This may be rather optimistic.

The pros and cons of going to mediation

Pros	Cons
• Can provide a cost-effective way of resolving a dispute, particularly where neither side can be sure of winning.	• Unless you are able to make use of a community scheme, you may find it expensive and the only way you will get the costs back is if your opponent agrees to pay them as part of any settlement you reach.
• Can assist reconciliation of the parties – precisely because there is no winner and no loser.	• If the mediation is unsuccessful, it will add further to the costs and delay of the case.
• Can provide a more flexible range of solutions.	• It may be exploited by one party who has no real interest in reaching a settlement but wants to test the strength of the other side's case and/or as a delaying tactic.
• Can be set up relatively quickly.	
• Is less formal than a court hearing.	
• All the discussion takes place on a 'without prejudice' basis. This means that if agreement cannot be reached and the case ultimately goes to trial, neither side can refer to the fact that mediation was attempted or what was said – or offered – during the negotiations.	

will usually pay. If the mediation fails and the case has to go to court, the judge will not usually order the losing side to pay the mediation costs.

Mediation, then, is not necessarily a cheap option. Nevertheless, it can provide a very effective way of resolving a dispute before significant legal costs have been incurred and both sides have become entrenched in their positions. It is not surprising, therefore, that mediation is actively encouraged by the courts, and even if matters cannot be resolved before proceedings are started, mediation can still be set up at any stage before the case comes to trial. In fact, the court will almost always be willing to halt the proceedings to allow time for the mediation to take place.

❝Mediation is not necessarily cheap, but it can be effective in resolving disputes before heavy costs are incurred and positions become entrenched.❞

25

Cases where mediation would not be appropriate

- Where there are good reasons for suspecting your opponent is not really interested in reaching an agreement or is unlikely to honour the terms of any agreement you might reach.
- In a case involving stalking or intimidation.
- Where it is necessary to obtain an order that the court will be able to enforce if it is not complied with – for example, an injunction to stop someone from causing noise nuisance.
- If your case is so good that you ought to be able to persuade the court to find in your favour without the need for a trial by ordering summary judgment at an early stage of the proceedings.
- If the deadline for starting court proceedings is about to expire (though this will not prevent you going to mediation after the case has been lodged at court).

“Mediation is not appropriate if your opponent isn't interested in reaching an agreement, or if your case is so strong the court is likely to order a summary judgment. ”

For more information, phone the National Mediation Helpline on 0845 6030809 or go to the website, www.mediationhelpline.com, which lists accredited mediation providers. If you are on benefits or a low income, you may be able to get free mediation through the Law Society's *pro bono* (free legal service) scheme. Ask at your local Citizens Advice Bureau for an application form.

How mediation works

Although the procedure is flexible and can be changed to suit the needs of those involved, most mediations include:

Opening statements

Everyone meets in the same room. There is an introduction by the mediator, and then each side is invited to make an opening statement. There is then an opportunity for anyone to ask questions before everyone goes to their own room.

Exploration of the issues

The mediator has a private meeting with each party and then goes between each of them exchanging information, discussing with each side what their expectations are and looking for common ground between them.

Negotiation

The mediator will want to lay the ground carefully and it may be some time before any proposals for settlement are discussed. At some stage the parties will meet up again to see where they have got to, discuss a particular issue or sticking point or – even better – discuss the possibility of settlement.

Settlement

If it becomes apparent that agreement can be reached, there will be more detailed discussions, either face to face or through the mediator, to agree the terms of the settlement. If an agreement is drawn up and signed, it will be regarded as a binding contract between the parties and can be enforced through the courts although the court will not be able to adjudicate on the original dispute.

ROUND TABLE MEETING

If both sides are legally represented, it may be possible to reach agreement without going through a formal mediation, with each party relying on their own lawyer to negotiate on their behalf. Of course, this can be done through correspondence but in some cases it is helpful for everyone to get together and see if they can hammer out an agreement. This will only work if there is a genuine willingness on each side to compromise. Once again, the meeting should take place somewhere where there is sufficient room for each party to be able to discuss matters comfortably and out of earshot of their opponent.

ARBITRATION

Arbitration is most commonly used in commercial and building disputes; often because the contract between the parties specifically provides for any dispute to be dealt with in that way. In fact, a full-scale arbitration is not unlike a trial with the arbitrator acting as the judge and listening to the evidence before making a decision that is binding on both sides. An arbitrator is chosen from a list of suitably qualified people and, as in mediation, both sides share the cost of setting up the arbitration.

The pros and cons of round table discussions

Pros	Cons
• All of those that apply to mediation (see page 25).	• You are dependent upon the negotiating skills of your lawyer.
• Cheaper than mediation as there is no mediator's fee and normally the meeting can take place in the offices of one of the lawyers.	• Without the help of an independent third party, the discussions may become bogged down in point scoring.

The pros and cons of arbitration

Pros	Cons
• Arbitration can usually be set up more quickly than a civil trial.	• The cost.
• The arbitrator will usually have a particular expertise in the area that is in dispute.	• If the dispute raises a complicated legal point, the arbitrator may not be able to deal with it properly.
• The procedure and hearing may be less formal.	

CRIMINAL INJURIES COMPENSATION AUTHORITY (CICA)

Although strictly speaking the CICA does not exist to provide an alternative to court action, it may sometimes provide a more effective means of getting compensation in personal injury cases than going through the courts. As its name suggests, its purpose is to compensate the victims of crime; however, in order to make a claim, there does not need to have been a criminal conviction, or even an arrest, as long as the CICA is satisfied that you have been on the receiving end of a criminal offence (usually an assault).

This scheme is particularly useful if you have suffered injury as a result of being assaulted at work (for example, if you're a teacher or social worker) for which your employer cannot be held responsible. You have two years to make a claim. The CICA will first consider your case on the basis of your paper application and supporting documents. If you are not happy with their decision, you can request a hearing and a panel will listen to any oral evidence and arguments you want them to consider before making a final decision.

❝ As long as the CICA believes you have suffered from a criminal offence causing personal injury, it should agree to compensation. ❞

The pros and cons of the CICA

Pros	Cons
• You will be able to get compensation, even if the person responsible for injuring you has no money.	• The amounts of compensation awarded are lower than in the civil court. • You will not be able to claim for the cost of using a lawyer to represent you.

 Full details of the scheme and the amounts of compensation awarded are available on the CICA website: www.cica.gov.uk.

WHY GO FOR ALTERNATIVE DISPUTE RESOLUTION?

ADR is not an easy option. By the time you are on the brink of, or involved in, court proceedings, it is likely that feelings are running high and it can be very difficult to step back and look at the bigger picture. Judges may complain about the amount of time and money wasted on taking cases to court that should have been settled long before, but they are looking at it from the point of view of an objective professional (which, of course, is what they are paid to be). It's very different to be directly involved in a dispute, which may touch on all sorts of issues that may be difficult to deal with on a personal level.

Nevertheless, it is important to try to keep an open mind to the possibility of reaching an agreement with your opponent at any stage in the proceedings. Try to avoid becoming so deeply entrenched in your position that you leave yourself no room for manoeuvre.

On a practical note, with the exception of arbitration, if you do try going down the ADR route and get nowhere, there is nothing to stop you from continuing to pursue your case through the courts. The trial judge will not be aware of any attempts to mediate or negotiate a settlement until after judgment has been given. So, even if you decide you don't want to use one of the more formal methods of ADR, you will have nothing to lose by exploring the possibility of reaching a compromise with your opponent.

> **" Try to consider the possibility of reaching agreement at any stage in the proceedings. "**

Making a claim: a checklist

✓ Do I have the type of case the civil courts deal with?

✓ Am I in time to bring a claim?

✓ What sort of court is likely to deal with my claim?

✓ What are the cost implications?

✓ Would I be able to get what I want through some alternative way of dispute resolution?

✓ If so, which one (or ones) might work best for my situation?

✓ Is there a good reason for not trying ADR?

Representation

No book can tell you if you have a strong case or not
- for that, you are going to need professional advice.
This section should help you decide where to go to
get advice and what it might cost.

Where to start

If you're on a tight budget or you know that you are unlikely to get damages of more than £5,000, your first priority will probably be to keep the cost of that advice as low as possible. There are a number of sources of free advice that will give you at least a preliminary idea of whether it is worth taking the case further.

CITIZENS ADVICE BUREAU (CAB)

The CAB will be able to give you an idea of whether you might be able to make or defend a civil claim. They should also be able to recommend solicitors in your local area that deal with your type of case. CAB advisers, though trained in advice work, are not legally qualified, so there will be a limit to how much help they can give, but they should be able to point you in the right direction.

> **"CAB advisers should be able to point you in the right direction regarding civil claims. Law Centres specialise in social welfare law. "**

LAW CENTRES

These are usually staffed by qualified lawyers and offer another source of free advice. They specialise in social welfare law, so if your problem is to do with housing, immigration, education, mental health or state benefits, then it may be worth finding out where your nearest Law Centre is (see box, below).

LEGAL HELP

If you are on state benefits or a low income, you may be able to make use of the Community Legal Services (CLS) Legal Help scheme, which is really a type of legal aid. To take advantage of the scheme you will need to go to a solicitor who is authorised by the CLS to advise on the kind of claim that you have. Although this might limit your choice, it does mean that any firm that does have a CLS franchise will have a degree of expertise in that area of the law.

 The Citizens Advice Bureau website is www.adviceguide.org.uk, where you can find lots of helpful information. To find your nearest Law Centre go to www.lawcentres.org.uk or telephone 020 7387 8570.

WHICH? LEGAL SERVICE

This is a subscription service. You can join it through the internet at www.whichlegalservice.co.uk. You pay £12.75 a quarter and this enables you to speak to legal advisers as you follow through your small claim. It is particularly helpful if you are using the small claims track as a litigant in person and need a little help as you progress.

USING THE INTERNET

The internet provides advertising space for any number of legal advisory services. For example, www.venables.co.uk contains links to the websites of solicitors and other organisations that offer a free initial advice by email. In fact, a quick search on the internet will throw up a large number of solicitors' firms and claims managers who offer a free or fixed price preliminary written or telephone advice or assessment of your case over the internet.

Although this can be a very convenient way of dipping your toe in the legal water, the quality of these services varies enormously and will not necessarily be provided by someone who is legally qualified. Bear in mind that any offer of free advice by a commercial firm is essentially a marketing ploy designed to attract potential clients by catching them early. Many of the firms who advertise in this way are well established and

Free advice from a solicitor

A lot of solicitors offer a free or fixed price initial consultation. To find out which solicitors near you offer this service you can go to the Community Legal Services website – www.clsdirect.org.uk – and search their database of solicitors.

❝ The quality of advice offered via the internet varies enormously and may not come from someone who is legally qualified. ❞

reputable, but inevitably there will be a few sharks swimming in among them. If you do decide to take up an offer of free or cheap advice over the internet, you can check the firm out on the Law Society website (see Finding a Solicitor on pages 35–41).

If 'free' advice is on offer, make sure that it stays free by not providing your credit card details. If you find the service you receive helpful and efficient, you may want to use it to pursue your claim, but if not, you should not feel under any pressure to do so. Making a preliminary enquiry does not commit you to that organisation or prevent you from looking for another lawyer who may suit your needs better.

The Community Legal Services website is www.clsdirect.org.uk and it has further information about Legal Help.

Researching the law yourself

If you are comfortable using the internet, there are several websites that will give you a brief summary of the law relating to various types of civil claim and procedure.

✓ Citizens Advice Bureau (www.adviceguide.org.uk): has information about small claims, using a solicitor, getting help with legal costs and personal injury claims.

✓ Community Legal Services (www.clsdirect.org.uk) also allows you to download information leaflets on dealing with debt, losing your home, 'no win no fee' actions, problems with goods and services, medical accidents, racial discrimination, personal injury, disability rights, neighbour and community disputes and mental health.

There are also several commercial legal service websites that provide summaries of the law on various topics:

✓ www.legalserviceshop.com has sections on personal injury, medical negligence, housing, employment and consumer law.

✓ www.legalzone.co.uk covers injunctions, personal injury and consumer disputes.

❝ While the internet is a helpful resource for going it alone, there are also many books that give valuable advice: see page 213 for suggestions. ❞

Finding a solicitor

Unless your claim is heading for the small claims track, sooner or later you will reach a stage when you will need to find a solicitor. The point at which you do this will vary from case to case.

You may reach the conclusion that you cannot move things on any further without professional help, or discover that your opponent has already been to see a solicitor. There are also some situations where you will need to take immediate steps to find legal representation, for example if:

- **The situation itself is urgent,** perhaps because you are being harassed or threatened with violence.
- **The time limit** for starting your claim is about to expire.
- **You are on the receiving end** of a solicitor's letter or formal letter of claim. Ignoring a formal letter of claim, or even putting off dealing with it for the time being, will only make things worse. You need proper advice about whether or not you might be liable.

Who you choose to act for you is probably one of the most important decisions you will make in relation to your claim. You will be dependent upon their professional skills to achieve the best result possible for you and at a personal level it is important that you should feel comfortable and able to discuss all aspects of your case with whoever is dealing with your claim.

Depending on how your case is being funded, your choice of solicitor may be limited. If you have legal expenses insurance (see page 48), the insurer may appoint a solicitor from a panel that the insurance company regularly uses. Similarly, trade unions tend to have an agreement with a particular firm of solicitors who they have a close working relationship with and who handle all the claims funded by the union. This may limit your choice and mean that your solicitor's office is on the other side of the country, but you may consider that to be an inconvenience you are willing to put up with if it means that you don't have to worry about finding the money to pay lawyers' fees.

The other advantage of these arrangements is that you can be

The time limits for different types of claim are covered in detail on page 13.

reasonably confident that the firm of solicitors appointed to take on your case is experienced in your type of claim. However, if you really do want to use another solicitor, once you reach the stage of starting court proceedings, your insurer cannot dictate who you use and you will have the final say about which solicitor handles the claim for you.

> **!** If your existing solicitor does not usually deal with civil claims, you might be better off simply asking him or her to recommend someone local who does.

THE MAIN OPTIONS

When it comes to deciding who to go to, these are the main options:

Your existing solicitor

You may have a solicitor who has worked for you in the past and who you get on well with. The advantage of going to him or her is that you will be using someone you know and trust. On the other hand, the solicitor who did such a good job on the conveyancing when you bought your house or who got you off that speeding ticket, may not have a particular experience in civil claims or the type of law that is involved in your case. One way around this would be for your solicitor to obtain advice from a barrister who does have the necessary expertise. The disadvantage of doing this is that you will be paying for two lawyers at a very early stage and if the case is, in fact, quite straightforward, you are

unlikely to recover the cost of using a barrister so early on in the proceedings.

Specialist firms

You should be able to find a firm of solicitors local to you that is experienced in handling civil claims. Alternatively, you may decide to try one of the very large firms of solicitors that have a national reputation for the type of work they do. These are usually based in a large city. If your case requires a specialist approach, you may want to consider using one of these, even if it means that you have to travel some distance whenever you need to see your solicitor. Inevitably, they are likely to be more expensive; being at the top of the tree in the legal profession means that your services don't come cheap, but for a few cases involving ground-breaking areas of law or very large sums of money they may be the best option.

 Look for solicitors that have Lexcel status. This is the Law Society's quality assurance mark and is only awarded to firms that meet high standards of client care and professional practice. The Bar Council (www.barcouncil.org.uk) operates a similar quality assurance scheme, Bar Mark, which is awarded to barristers' chambers rather than individual barristers.

Where to look

The main places to look for a solicitor to advise you are:

The Law Society website (www.lawsociety.org.uk)

The 'Find a Solicitor' section on the website has a full list of solicitors' firms in England and Wales. You can refine your search to the type of law and area of the country you are looking in. It also indicates which firms have been awarded Lexcel status (see box at the foot of the page opposite) and those that are accredited members of its personal injury, clinical negligence, Mental Health Review Tribunal and civil and commercial mediation panels.

The Community Legal Services website (www.clsdirect.org.uk)

There is also a step-by-step guide to finding a legal adviser on this website, listing solicitors both by location and practice areas and indicating those that offer a free initial consultation.

Legal directories

These are helpful, particularly if you do want to go for one of the big specialist firms. The two leading directories are Chambers UK and Legal 500. They are both published in book form and should be available in your local reference library or you can go to their websites: www.chambersandpartners.com and www.legal500.com. The directories are particularly useful because they identify solicitors (and barristers) with a particular expertise by name.

High street solicitor or large specialist firm?

Here are some of the pros of each:

High street
- Lower overheads, so cheaper to use.
- Offer a more personal service – you're more likely to deal with your legal adviser in face-to-face meetings rather than over the telephone.
- Convenience of location.

Specialist firm
- High level of specialist experience and expertise with excellent back-up from an in-house team.
- Pulling power – having one of the big names in the legal world acting for you is likely to give you an advantage in dealing with your opponent, particularly when negotiating a settlement.

Claims managers

Claims managers (also known as claims handlers) deal with straightforward personal injury and accident claims. They make their money by taking on low risk claims on a conditional fee basis (see page 42) and settling them quickly. If you have been the victim of a rear-end shunt, they will be pleased to hear from you, but if your story is rather more complicated, it may be a different matter.

It is difficult to think of a good reason for using a claims manager. If you have a straightforward personal injury claim which can be settled quickly, you won't have any difficulty finding a solicitor to take it on. You'll get a more personal service from a solicitor, and you may well get more damages because the insurer on the other side will know that they are dealing with someone who is able to take the claim to court if necessary. Some claims managers offer to pay the premium for the insurance that you will

need to take out in case you lose, but the cost of the premium should be paid as part of any settlement. If you really have difficulty raising the money for the premium upfront and your case is clear-cut, you can probably come to an arrangement with your solicitor to pay in instalments or make a deferred payment.

On the other hand, there are a number of disadvantages in using a claims manager:

- Claims managers do not use legally qualified advisers, so the quality of the advice you receive can be variable.
- Unlike solicitors, who are regulated by the Law Society, claims managers are not subject to strict regulation.
- The only funding option you will be offered is a conditional fee agreement (see box, below) regardless of whether you already have legal expenses insurance (see page 48) or may be eligible for legal aid (see pages 46–7).
- If the claim cannot be settled, claims managers are not able to issue proceedings on your behalf, so they have to refer the case on to a solicitor (of their choice).
- You may be advised to accept a lower amount of compensation than your claim is actually worth in order to ensure that the claims manager gets their costs.

 If you do decide to use a claims manager, make sure that he or she is registered with the Claims Standards Council (www.claims council.org.uk) and steer well clear of any organisation that asks you to pay a contingency fee – a fee that is taken out of any damages you may get.

 A conditional fee agreement is an arrangement whereby lawyers act for a client on a 'no win no fee' basis. Information on this subject is given on pages 42-5.

Claims farmers

Claims farmers take things one stage further than claims managers. They 'cultivate' claims by approaching people who may have never thought about making a claim. They are particularly active in housing disrepair cases where they will target a run-down housing estate and go round like door-to-door salespeople knocking on doors to drum up business. If you have been alerted to the possibility that you might have a claim by one of their salespeople, you are almost certainly better off going to see a local solicitor.

Solicitor or barrister?

Although there is some overlap in the work they do, solicitors and barristers usually have quite separate parts to play in preparing and presenting your case. This means if the claim goes to trial, you will probably need both a solicitor and a barrister.

- Solicitors deal with clients in the first instance. They give advice throughout the case, deal with all the correspondence, liaise with insurers and the court, and conduct negotiations on behalf of their client. They are responsible for making sure that everything necessary to get the claim ready for trial has been done. Sometimes they also present the case to the court, but this is more usually done by barristers. They usually run their business as a partnership (the large firms will have hundreds of partners).

Jargon buster

Advocate Lawyer (either solicitor or barrister) who presents a case in court

Barrister Lawyer specialising in advice and advocacy

Instruct Employ a lawyer or expert to act for you

Legal executive Someone who has experience of legal work and/or qualifications obtained through the Institute of Legal Executives (ILEX). Some legal executives go on to qualify as solicitors

Paralegal Someone who does not have a legal qualification but who has some experience in legal work and may be employed to deal with civil claims

Queens Counsel (QC) senior barrister

Solicitor A fully qualified and trained lawyer whose professional work is regulated by the Law Society who deals with the day-to-day conduct of the claim

Trainee solicitor Someone who has passed all the solicitors' exams and is now working under supervision under a two-year training contract to become fully qualified

❝If a claims farmer tells you that you might have a claim, you are most probably better off going to see a local solicitor.❞

- **Barristers** usually become involved later on in the case. They are often asked to give specialist advice on the more difficult legal aspects of the claim and draft the court documents. Their main role is to present the case at trial. From the start of their career, barristers specialise in court work, learning to put forward legal arguments and present the evidence in the best possible light for their client. Barristers are self-employed but they usually work together, sharing premises and administrative services, known as chambers. Usually you cannot take your case directly to a barrister. You will need a solicitor to instruct a barrister on your behalf. However, some barristers can now accept work directly from clients; this is known as 'public access' work (see box, below).

Ask the expert

What does a solicitor charge?

One reason why you may be happy to have someone who is not a solicitor dealing with your claim, is that this will be reflected in the lower fees charged for their time. Your solicitor's costs will be based on the time taken to work on your case, charged at an hourly rate. The hourly rate is set according to the level of legal professional concerned. Often the work can be split so that a solicitor will deal with the more complicated aspects of the claim and someone more junior will do the more routine jobs.

If you need to get a report from an expert or to use a barrister, their fees will appear as 'disbursements' on your solicitor's bill and these can add significantly to the costs. In addition, if there are court proceedings, you will also have to pay court fees (see page 63).

❛❛ 'Disbursements', such as reports from experts and the services of a barrister, can add significantly to the cost of a claim. ❜❜

 A list of those barristers who are able to do public access work and the kind of cases they specialise in is available on the Bar Council website, www.barcouncil.org.uk.

Solicitors' fees

This table sets out the recommended hourly rates for solicitors for their work. Each town or city in England falls into a particular band and the places in the table are designed to illustrate the range of fees you might have to pay, depending on where your solicitor is based.

Place	Grade A	Grade B	Grade C	Grade D
City of London	£380	£274	£210	£129
Central London	£292	£222	£181	£116
Rest of London	£210-£246	£158-£210	£152	£111
Band 1 (including Manchester, Leeds and Liverpool)	£195	£173	£145	£116
Band 2 (including Bath, Cheltenham and Cambridge)	£183	£161	£131	£101
Band 3 (including Devon and Cornwall)	£167	£150	£128	£95

Key

Grade A Solicitors with more than eight years litigation experience

Grade B Solicitors or legal executives with more than four years litigation experience

Grade C Solicitors or legal executives with less than four years experience

Grade D Paralegals or trainee solicitors

To find out the going rate for solicitors' fees for your local area, go to
www.hmscourts-service/publications/guidance/scco/appendix.2.htm

Funding your claim

One of the first and most important things your solicitor will discuss with you is how you are going to fund your claim. There are a number of options although in practice you may find that your choice is limited by individual circumstances and the type of claim you have.

NO WIN NO FEE: CONDITIONAL FEE AGREEMENTS

The most common way of funding a civil claim is by a conditional fee agreement (CFA). Under a CFA your solicitor agrees to work on a 'no win no fee' basis. If the case succeeds, he or she will be entitled to a success fee. If you lose, your solicitor won't be paid anything. The success fee is calculated as a percentage of the solicitor's costs. The greater the risk, the higher the percentage or 'uplift' the solicitor will be able to claim as a success fee. The idea is that the success fees pay for any unsuccessful CFA cases that your solicitor takes on.

Assessing the risk

In order to decide whether to take the case and, if so, what the success fee should be, the first thing your solicitor will do is a risk assessment. This involves trying to predict the outcome of the case. Unless the claim is assessed as having a better than 50 per cent chance of success, your solicitor will not take it on. The consequence of losing a CFA case, and with it the prospect of receiving no payment for hours of work, means that most solicitors will err on the side of caution when carrying out the risk assessment. Even if you have a good arguable case, if it raises, for example, legal arguments that are not clear cut, you will find it difficult to get a solicitor to act for you under a CFA.

The original assessment may also need to be revised as the claim progresses. The prospect of success can both improve and get worse. An employer's negligence claim that initially

❝The risk assessment calculates the likely chance of success. If this is under 50 per cent, the solicitor won't take it on. ❞

 Other ways of funding your claim are potentially legal aid (see pages 46-7), paying privately (see page 48), legal expenses insurance (also see page 48), your trade union (if you are a member) or through *pro bono* representation (see page 49).

appeared to be uncertain, may result in an early admission of liability by a defendant who knows that there have been previous similar accidents, which will make the claim difficult to defend. On the other hand, your rear-shunt claim may become less attractive if there is an independent witness who says you were reversing at the time the collision took place.

is probably because it is easier to predict the outcome of a personal injury claim than many other types of civil claim, making it easier for lawyers to make an accurate assessment of the risk involved in taking on the case.

Who can use a CFA?

Although it is usually the claimant who has a CFA, there is no reason why you should not be able to arrange one if you are defending the claim and your chance of succeeding is good. CFAs are still used most often in personal injury claims. This

❝There is no reason why someone defending a claim can't use a CFA, which are most often used in personal injury claims. ❞

Conditional fee agreements: the hidden costs

You may not have to pay your solicitor's costs if you lose the case, but there are other expenses that you may have to pay:

- Insurance to cover paying your opponent's costs if you lose. This is known as an 'after the event' policy (ATE) and usually involves a one-off premium. A policy in a personal injury or housing disrepair case will probably cost a few hundred pounds, but if your claim is a contractual or professional negligence case, it is likely to be much higher.
- Expert reports, if they are needed. Unlike lawyers, expert witnesses are not allowed to work on a 'no win no fee' basis.
- Any shortfall in the costs that your opponent is ordered to pay. If you win your case, the success fee, the insurance premium and the cost of using an expert can all be claimed back as part of your costs. However, if the judge assessing the amount of costs to be paid decides that they are too high, he or she may refuse to allow the full amount.

This means that although a CFA is much cheaper than paying privately for a solicitor, it does not come free of charge.

Negotiating a settlement under a CFA

The other side will know that you are funding the claim by a CFA, but not the level at which the success fee has been set; so they will not be aware of how your solicitor assesses the risk. Problems can arise if your opponent makes an offer of settlement that falls a long way short of what you were hoping to get but your solicitor and the insurer want you to accept it.

It is often extremely difficult to predict the result if the case goes all the way to trial. A lot will depend on which judge you get, how your opponent's witnesses

Ask the expert

I am suing my insurance broker for negligently advising me to opt out of my company pension scheme in favour of a personal pension plan. He denies that he ever gave me that advice and there is nothing in writing but obviously I would not have acted as I did if he hadn't told me a personal pension was better. I am using a CFA and my solicitor has assessed the chance of success as being 60 per cent. It will cost about £55,000 to make good the loss I have suffered. The other side has offered £20,000, which my solicitor has advised me to accept. I'm sure we would win if we went to trial and I'm willing to take the risk, but it seems that my solicitor is not. She has told me that if I don't take the money, not only will she not be willing to carry on with the case but that the ATE insurer also wants to pull out. Generally I get on well with my solicitor and I don't really want to go to someone else. What are my options?

A 60 per cent chance of success means that there is a 40 per cent chance that you will lose. This makes it a relatively high-risk claim – probably this is because if the case goes to trial, it will be your word against that of your broker. If you really want to carry on with the claim, the first option is to continue to use your current solicitor but as a privately paying client. This means that it will be you rather than your solicitor and the insurance company who is taking the financial risk of refusing the offer.

The only way you can continue to protect yourself against paying costs if you lose, is to find another solicitor who is willing to take over the CFA, which you may find difficult. Otherwise, you could do the case yourself, but you will need to think very carefully about whether this is something you want to take on. It will take a lot of time and if you lose the case, you will have to pay the costs from the time you took over from your solicitor. If you do decide to do it yourself, you might want to see if you can come to an arrangement with your solicitor under which you do most of the work but you pay her to help out with some of the more difficult things.

give their evidence: things that your solicitor simply cannot know in advance. Even if you win on liability, you may still not get the full amount of damages you are claiming.

If a low offer is accepted, your solicitor will recover the costs of the work done so far and a success fee. In addition, the insurer who has provided the ATE policy will be off the hook. These can be very powerful incentives for persuading you to settle your claim for less than it is worth, even after allowing for the risks of litigation.

Most lawyers advising clients in this situation will want the best outcome possible for their client and will take pains to ensure that they give objective advice. But there are a few who may be less scrupulous about encouraging acceptance of an offer that is too low. However, since continuing with a CFA case after a not completely unreasonable offer has been made constitutes a significant commercial risk to your solicitor, it is almost inevitable that a cautious approach to the case will be taken by those advising you.

Conditional fee agreements: points to remember

- You must tell your solicitor about any insurance policy you have which may cover your legal expenses. If it turns out there was an alternative way of funding the claim, your solicitor will not be entitled to a success fee.
- Before you sign the CFA, your solicitor should spend some time explaining how the agreement works and what you will be expected to pay. If the charges seem high, you can always shop around to see if you can get a better deal.
- If you need a barrister, he or she will also work under a CFA to cover the cost of the work they do and will also carry out a risk assessment of your claim. If the barrister refuses the case, even if your solicitor is willing to go on with it, this may mean that the insurer is not willing to back the claim.
- 'Success' does not necessarily mean going all the way to trial and winning. It may mean settling the case on what your lawyers advise you are the best terms possible.
- Your obligations under the CFA will include replying promptly to queries and requests for information and being open and honest with your solicitor about anything that is relevant to the claim. If you do not do this, you are liable to find yourself without the benefit of a CFA or legal representation.
- Don't forget that if you are on the other side of someone who has a CFA, if you lose the case you will be paying the success fee and the cost of the ATE on top of their legal costs.

LEGAL AID

Legal aid (also known as public funding) means that all or part of the cost of your legal expenses is met by the state. Legal aid is no longer available for many civil claims, including personal injury, property and contract disputes. You can still get it for claims involving clinical negligence, housing problems, mental health and judicial review. However, the service has been franchised so that you can only use a law firm that has been approved for your type of claim.

The pros and cons of legal aid

Pros	Cons
• You will either make a relatively small contribution to your legal costs or pay nothing at all.	• It is very difficult to get legal aid (see box, opposite).
• If you lose, you won't have to pay your opponent's costs unless the court decides you can afford it. In practice, this usually means that unless there is a dramatic improvement in your financial situation, no one will expect you to pay anything.	• If you don't get your costs off your opponent, unless it would cause you serious hardship, you must pay them back out of any damages you receive. This is known as the 'statutory charge'. It is possible to postpone payment if you are using the money to buy a house to live in.
	• In some areas there is a shortage of solicitors who do legal aid work such as mental health and housing, so you may have difficulty finding a solicitor.

The pros and cons of privately paying

Pros	Cons
• You have complete freedom to choose which solicitor you go to.	• You have no protection against having to pay your opponent's costs if you lose the case. This will include the success fee and ATE premium if he or she is on a CFA.
• You always have the final say in how the claim is conducted, including any settlement negotiations.	• If you win but your opponent has legal aid, it is extremely unlikely that you will get your costs back.
• You do not have to worry about having to make up any shortfall in a success fee if the claim succeeds.	• Even if you win against an opponent who can afford to pay, you may not get all your costs back – the court will not make your opponent pay costs that are considered to be too high.

Can I get legal aid?

1 | Is my claim in one of the categories that still get legal aid?

These are clinical negligence, housing, mental health and judicial review.

2 | Do I qualify financially?

If you are on income support or jobseeker's allowance, or you receive pension credit, you will be financially eligible for legal aid. Children also usually qualify as their parents' income is not taken into account. If you don't fall into these categories, your income and that of your partner will be assessed. If you have capital in excess of £8,000 or a joint gross income of more than £2,350 a month, you won't be eligible. The Community Legal Services website – www.cls-direct.org.uk – has a financial calculator that will do the arithmetic for you.

3 | Is my case good enough?

If your claim is for damages, you will have to satisfy the cost /benefit test:

The chance of success is very good (better than 80 per cent)	If you win, you will get more damages than the cost of bringing the claim
The chance of success is good (60-80 per cent)	If you win, you will get at least twice as much in damages as the cost of bringing the claim
The chance of success is moderate (50-60 per cent)	If you win, you will get at least four times as much in damages as the cost of bringing the claim

If your claim is not for damages, the remedy you are seeking has to be 'proportionate', in other words, it must justify the cost of the claim.

❝If you have capital of over £8,000 or a joint gross monthly income of more than £2,350, you can't get legal aid.❞

PRIVATELY PAYING

If you want to avoid the restrictions of a CFA and you can afford it, you could simply opt to pay your own costs and hope to recover them from your opponent if you win the case. At the outset, your solicitor should discuss the implications of doing this and give you an estimate of what the costs are likely to be. You will normally be asked to pay a lump sum upfront and you should receive an account at least every six months.

> " Your solicitor should check any legal expenses insurance policy early on to identify any potential problems with it. "

LEGAL EXPENSES INSURANCE

Legal expenses insurance (sometimes referred to as 'before the event' insurance or BTE) can either be free-standing or attached to a car or house insurance policy. It will usually pay both your legal expenses and the other side's costs if you lose. However, you remain the one theoretically responsible for paying your solicitor's fees and you may actually have to do so if there is any problem with the policy and the insurance company refuses to pay up. Your solicitor should check the policy and renewal notices at the outset so that any potential problems can be picked up early. The insurance company will only support the claim if you are likely to win. Your solicitor will have to report to them on a regular basis to confirm that this is still the case.

The pros and cons of legal expenses insurance

Pros	Cons
• You should be fully protected from having to pay either your costs or the other side's costs if you lose. • You will not have to pay an ATE premium or the cost of obtaining expert evidence.	• You may end up using a solicitor chosen by the insurance company who is not based near to where you live. • If the insurance company thinks you have not co-operated with your solicitor or that you have concealed something relevant to the claim, it can withdraw cover. • It is the insurance company who will decide how far the claim should go. If your solicitor or barrister advise that an offer should be accepted or that the claim is unlikely to succeed, the insurance company will probably accept that advice and refuse to fund the claim further.

TRADE UNION

If you are a member of a trade union you may find that the union will support your claim and pay your opponent's costs if you lose the case. The only disadvantage is that you won't have any choice about which solicitor you go to. The union will have an arrangement with a particular firm of solicitors, in effect bulk buying their services, usually by way of collective conditional fee agreements, although you won't have to buy ATE insurance.

PRO BONO REPRESENTATION

Both the Law Society (for solicitors) and the Bar Council (for barristers) sometimes can arrange for solicitors or barristers to take on cases for which they don't get paid. This is known as 'pro bono' work. To qualify, you will have to show that there is no other way of funding your claim, such as by legal aid or a conditional fee agreement. The fact that you are not paying your lawyer will not protect you from having to pay your opponent's costs if you lose.

To apply, you need to submit a written application (the Citizens Advice Bureau or a Law Centre will help you with this). Your case will then be considered by a senior barrister or solicitor and, if it is approved, efforts will be made to find

Jargon buster

ADR (Alternative Dispute Resolution) The various ways available to sort out a dispute instead of going to court

ATE (After the event) (insurance) A policy taken out after the event leading to the claim, which insures against the risk of losing the claim and having to pay the other side's costs

BTE (Before the event) (insurance) A legal expenses insurance policy that was in place before the event leading to the claim

CFA (Conditional Fee Agreement) An agreement where a solicitor agrees to act in a civil claim. If the claim succeeds, the solicitor gets a 'success fee'. If it fails, he or she doesn't get paid at all

CLS (Community Legal Services) An offshoot of the government department responsible for making low-cost legal advice and representation available – mostly through legal aid

CPR (Civil Procedure Rules) The court rules that apply to civil claims

ILEX (Institute of Legal Executives) The body responsible for training and regulating legal executives

someone suitably qualified to do the case for you. There is no guarantee, even if your case is approved, that you will be able to find someone willing to take it. The Law Society estimates that they are able to find a solicitor for about 75 per cent of the cases that are approved. Allocating the case takes about eight weeks.

 For more information about *pro bono* representation, go to www.lawworks.org.uk (solicitors) or www.barprobono.org.uk (barristers).

If things go wrong

Most people have a good working relationship with their lawyer, but sometimes things do go wrong and it is important to try to sort them out as quickly as possible. The court and your opponent won't know or make allowances for the fact that behind the scenes the relationship between you and your legal representative is on the verge of collapse

A lot of problems can be avoided if your solicitor, as should happen, writes to you every time you talk, confirming what was said and setting out what steps are to be taken. If your solicitor's recollection is different from yours, you should query this immediately, particularly if you do not agree with the suggested course of action. No offer of settlement or attempt at negotiation should ever be made without first obtaining your express agreement, preferably in writing, to what is proposed.

If things do go wrong during the court proceedings (for example, if a deadline is missed), it is important that you receive a full explanation about what happened and why. You should be told what steps will be taken to put matters right, and if the mistake has incurred extra costs, whose responsibility they will be.

CODES OF PROFESSIONAL CONDUCT

Both solicitors and barristers have codes of professional conduct, which they are expected to follow. Even if the person advising you is not a solicitor, the firm he or she works for will be run by solicitors, so the code should be complied with. The solicitor's code has detailed rules about client care (see box, below).

❝ Your solicitor should put in writing confirmation of any conversations you have. If it doesn't match your recollection, say so. ❞

 The solicitor's code of conduct is available online at www.sra.org.uk and there is a guide to the code on the Law Society website: www.lawsociety.org.uk. The code for barristers is available on the Bar Council's website: www.barcouncil.org.uk.

Steps to ... making a complaint

1   Start by writing to your solicitor, setting out your concerns and asking for an explanation. Try to keep an open mind at this stage as there may be a simple explanation, which will put your mind at rest.

2   If you do not get a satisfactory response, every solicitor's firm is required to have a complaints procedure and you should ask for details of it. Normally it will involve taking your complaint to a senior member of the firm. It may be possible to resolve your complaint within the firm, perhaps by someone else taking over the claim for you. You may be offered some form of mediation.

3   If you are still not satisfied that your matter has been dealt with properly, the next step is to take the complaint to the solicitors' professional body, the Law Society (or Bar Council if your complaint is about a barrister). Details of how to complain either about a solicitor or a barrister are available on the Law Society and Bar Council web sites (see opposite below).

4   If you are unhappy with the way in which your complaint is investigated by the professional body involved, you can refer the case to the Legal Services Ombudsman (see Useful addresses, pages 210-12). The Ombudsman can only investigate how the complaint was dealt with, and not whether your original complaint was justified.

5   If you remain convinced that the service you received was negligent and that you have suffered financial loss as a result, you might want to take legal advice about whether you could sue the firm for professional negligence. On the other hand, you may have had enough of the civil courts by then.

CHANGING YOUR SOLICITOR

If you are really unhappy with the quality of the service you've received, there is nothing to stop you from going to another law firm at any point right up to the final hearing. You do not have to wait until you have exhausted all the complaints procedures. Indeed, if you are already in the middle of taking a claim through the courts you need to make the change as soon as possible. There may

be funding implications that your new solicitor will be able to advise you about. In particular, if you are a privately paying client, your former solicitors will not release your file until they have been paid up to date. Likewise, if you have a CFA, your new solicitor must be willing to take the case on. If you want to keep the same barrister, you should be able to do so and you will also probably have to stick with any experts who have already written reports on your case.

CHALLENGING THE BILL

If your solicitor has kept you fully informed about the costs of the claim, there should be no nasty surprises when the bill arrives. If you are a privately paying client, you will receive interim bills as the case progresses. If you are concerned that you are being charged too much, you should raise it at the time you receive the interim bill. However, it is probably sensible to continue paying the interim bills under protest. They are unlikely to come to more than the final bill – even if you do get a reduction – and you will nevertheless have an opportunity to challenge the charges at the end of the case.

What you should do, however, is to ask for a detailed breakdown of the bill, which you are entitled to as long as you ask for it within three months. If you cannot reach agreement with your solicitor, you can ask the court to assess what it is reasonable for you to pay. You must wait until the end of the case to do this (see also the box, below).

If, at the end of the case, you still cannot agree the bill, you may want to ask a costs draftsman to check it for you (see page 180). However, you will need to pay him or her to do this for you.

❝ You are entitled to a breakdown of your solicitor's bill up to three months after you are billed. You can ask the court to assess what cost would be reasonable. ❞

 If your case has not involved court proceedings, you may be able to query the bill by using the remuneration procedure available through www.legalcomplaints.org.uk. This is a free service in which your bill can be checked to see if it is reasonable.

Going it alone

If your claim is worth less than £5,000 (or £1,000 for a personal injury or housing disrepair case), you can almost certainly manage your claim without the help of a lawyer.

The other, more difficult, situation where you might have to consider representing yourself is if you cannot find anyone to take your claim under a CFA and have no other way of paying for a lawyer. This situation can arise either right at the outset when you are unable to find a solicitor to accept the case or during the course of the proceedings if your existing lawyer decides that the risk has become too great to go any further.

WHAT IT INVOLVES

Either way, you need to be realistic about what being a litigant in person involves if you have a fast track or multi track claim:

- **Dealing promptly** with all correspondence (including letters that are from your opponent or your opponent's lawyers).
- **Dealing with the court documentation** and liaising with court staff – usually by telephone – to make sure that you have done everything that you need to do.
- **Organising and copying documents** that are relevant to your case.
- **Preparing witness statements** for yourself and anyone else who is giving evidence in support of your case.

- **If you need expert evidence,** finding and paying for an expert to prepare a report.
- **Going to court** to deal with any interim applications.
- **Researching the law.**
- **Preparing and presenting** your case at trial.

THE COST

In addition, you must take a long hard look at the risk you are running on costs. Don't allow yourself to think that this is something you can put off until later if and when the need arises. The reality of the situation is that if you cannot find a solicitor who will do the case under a CFA, your claim has already been assessed by the professionals as being high risk. You have to think about what an order to pay your opponent's costs would actually mean to you and whether that is, literally, the price that you are prepared to pay.

Probably the most difficult thing about being a litigant in person is not the amount of work it takes, but remaining sufficiently objective. Yet this is precisely what you must do if you want the court to take you seriously. However angry and frustrated you feel, it is vital that when you reply to letters or present your case to the court, you control your feelings and concentrate on making the points you need to as calmly as possible. If you get used to dealing with your claim in this way throughout the proceedings, you should find it much easier to present your case at trial in an objective manner, which is far more likely to impress the judge and get you the result you want.

GETTING HELP

The main sources of information if you are doing the claim yourself are:

- **The Civil Procedure Rules and Practice Directions** provide chapter and verse on taking a claim through the civil courts (see page 202).
- **Court staff will be able to give practical advice** about what you need to do. Never be afraid to telephone the court that is dealing with your claim to ask for help.
- **Your opponent's solicitors** are under a duty to co-operate with you in getting the case ready for trial. Obviously they cannot give you legal advice about your claim, but you can ask them to explain anything about court procedure that you are not sure about and they may be able to help in practical ways; for example, photocopying documents and the court bundle. Although they are acting for your opponent, their first duty is to the court. It is extremely unlikely that they will try to take advantage of you and you may find that you can have a reasonable working relationship with them, even though they are representing your opponent.

- **Even if you are doing most of the work yourself,** there is no reason why you shouldn't use a solicitor (or barrister through the public access scheme – see page 40) to help from time to time or to advise you on a specific procedural or legal point. You'll have to pay for the services they provide, but if you win your case, you'll be entitled to claim the cost from your opponent. This is sometimes known as unbundling.

You should also find that the information in this book gives you an understanding of what is involved in taking a civil claim through the courts. The section on the small claims track (see pages 84–98) deals with preparing and presenting your case to a judge; and practical advice for those who may not have legal representation is included where necessary throughout the book.

❝Making your points calmly and objectively is the best way to impress the judge and get the result you want.❞

Getting started

This chapter looks at what is involved in getting the claim off the ground – from gathering together relevant information to what you need to do to start proceedings. If you are defending a claim, this chapter also looks at how to deal with the initial paperwork.

Investigating the claim

If you are using a legal adviser allocated to you by an insurance company, your first contact is likely to be by telephone. Otherwise, if it is practical for you to do so, it is probably a good idea to go in to the solicitor's office to meet whoever is going to be dealing with your case. Either way, you will need to get ready all the information that you have relating to your claim.

WHAT TO TAKE TO THE FIRST MEETING

Your solicitor will want to have as much detail about the background of your case as possible. In order to help him or her advise you properly and make further enquiries on your behalf, you can:

- **Prepare a chronology** or sequence of events, setting everything out in the order in which it happened along with the date on which it occurred.
- **Make a list** of the names, addresses and telephone numbers of anybody who may be able and willing to act as a witness for you.
- **Collect together** any documents, including letters and photographs (if in a car accident), that relate to your claim.
- **If you think you might be eligible for legal aid,** make a note of your income and, if you are living with someone, that of your partner.
- **If you think your claim may be covered** by legal expenses insurance under a motor or household policy, have a copy of the policy to hand.

- **Make a list of all the questions** you want to ask.
- **If your opponent has a solicitor,** make a note of their name and where they are based.

It will already be obvious that the paperwork, even for a simple claim, can be extensive. It is a good idea to keep it together in a file so that everything you need is to hand.

MEETING YOUR LAWYER

The person dealing with your claim will not necessarily be a solicitor. It is not unusual for civil litigation to be conducted by a legal executive or experienced paralegal. If you are worried that they are not senior enough, you should raise this at an early stage. The easiest way of doing this is to find out who is in charge of civil litigation at the firm and write to them explaining the nature of your claim and setting out your concerns. Even if your legal adviser is not a qualified solicitor, he or she will be working under the supervision of somebody who is and, in the vast majority of cases, you can be confident that the person advising you knows what he or she is doing. So as long as you feel happy with the service and advice you are receiving, the fact that your 'solicitor' is not, in fact, a solicitor should not be a problem.

After the first meeting you should receive a letter setting out in detail the information about costs, who will handle your case and what will happen next, which should have been discussed during your meeting. If you have any doubts, then it might be sensible to look for someone else at this stage as a change of solicitor later on can be very disruptive.

WHAT HAPPENS NEXT

Your solicitor will now need to collect as much information as possible about your claim, not only from you, but also from documents relating to the claim and any witnesses who are able to support your account of what happened.

It may also be necessary to get an expert's report. For example, if your claim is for clinical negligence, you will need a senior doctor from the same field of medicine as the one who treated you to say whether the treatment you received was negligent. This will all take some time, so unless your case is straightforward or very urgent, it may feel as if nothing much is happening for a while. However, it is necessary to do this

right at the beginning; partly so that your solicitor can make a realistic assessment of whether you have a good case and partly because when your solicitor does approach the other side, he or she will need to put as much information as possible in the letter to the other side setting out your case.

Once the investigations are complete, and providing they support your case, your solicitor will be ready to put together all the information in support of your case in a formal letter of claim or response (see below).

Checking the facts

Before the formal letter of claim or response is sent out, it is absolutely vital that you check that it is factually correct. This means not only that the facts contained in it are correct but also that nothing important has been left out. Your solicitor will have been relying on his or her notes and may inadvertently have got something wrong or forgotten to write something down. If there are factual errors in the letter of claim or response and the case goes to trial, you can be sure they will come back to haunt you in cross-examination; when it will be suggested that you have changed your story.

If anything, this is even more important if you are doing the case yourself. When any inconsistencies are pointed out to you in cross-examination, you won't be able to say that your solicitor must have made a mistake.

For more information on experts' reports, see pages 130-8.

PRE-ACTION PROTOCOLS

The Civil Procedure Rules encourage the parties to a civil claim to be as open as possible with one another right from the beginning. This is initially achieved through a letter of claim, which is subsequently answered by a letter of response (see opposite page).

Most types of civil claim have a pre-action protocol (see box, right), which is a plan of action for exchanging information and narrowing the issues in dispute before court proceedings have even begun.

- If your claim falls into one of the categories that has a pre-action protocol, unless the time for starting court action is about to expire, you should follow the procedure set out in the protocol.
- If you don't, you are giving the other side a tactical advantage because they will be able to point to the fact that you have apparently ignored the protocol and rushed in to taking court action, which will not endear you to the court.
- If, in fact, using the pre-action protocol would have saved time and money in the main court proceedings, the court is likely to show its disapproval by ordering you to pay any costs that have been wasted as a result.
- You will also be criticised if your formal court documents put forward different arguments from those that were used in your protocol letter of claim or response.

Pre-action protocols

The following types of claim have pre-action protocols:

- Building and engineering disputes
- Defamation (libel and slander)
- Disease and illness cases
- Housing disrepair
- Judicial review (challenging a decision made by a public authority)
- Medical negligence
- Personal injury
- Professional negligence (accountants, architects, surveyors, solicitors, financial advisers, etc.)

You will find the pre-action protocols on the Ministry of Justice website: www.justice.gov.uk.

- Click 'What we do' on the home page. This will take you to a site index.
- Click 'civil procedure rules' and then choose pre-action protocols from the menu at the top.

The protocols are also in Volume 1 of the *White Book* or *Green Book* (see page 16), which you should be able to find at your local reference library.

Each protocol has a specimen letter of claim that can easily be adapted to your individual case.

There are also guidance notes to help you.

HOW THE PROTOCOLS WORK

The protocols set out exactly what information each party must supply to the other – starting with a letter of claim, which is answered by a letter of response – together with the timescale for doing so.

Letter of claim

The claimant sends a formal letter of claim, which should contain all the information that the defendant needs to investigate the claim and understand what the claimant is looking for by way of remedy. If the claimant wants financial compensation, there should be sufficient information for the defendant to calculate approximately how much. The letter of claim should include:

- **Sufficient information** about the claimant for the defendant to be able to identify who it is that is making the claim.
- **A clear summary of the facts** (a chronology is sometimes required and is nearly always helpful).
- **The basis on which the claim is made** – the legal wrong complained of, for example, negligence or breach of an agreement.
- **Why the claimant says that the defendant is responsible** – what he or she has done wrong or what he or she has failed to do.
- **A description of the damage suffered** by the claimant and what he or she wants the defendant to do to put matters right.

Depending on the type of protocol, there are also requirements relating to relevant documents which the claimant may want to see and choice of an expert if one is needed.

❝ If the claimant wants financial compensation, there should be sufficient information for the defendant to calculate approximately how much. ❞

Letter of response

The protocols allow defendants a specified time to investigate the claim and write a formal letter of response. This varies from 14 days in a defamation case to three months in a personal injury or clinical negligence claim. It is not unusual for defendants to ask for more time if they cannot complete their investigations within the time allowed. This may not be unreasonable if the claim is complicated or the defendant is having difficulty tracing an important witness. However, there should always be a good reason for giving the defendant more time and a clear time limit should always be set. Otherwise, in general terms, the letter of response should:

- **Say what facts are agreed** and what facts are in dispute.
- **If liability is admitted,** say so.
- **If part of the claim is admitted,** clearly identify which part.
- **If liability is denied,** the defendant should reply to the specific allegations that the claimant has made, explaining why they are rejected.
- **If the defendant needs further information,** say precisely what is needed.
- **If the claimant has suggested expert evidence is needed,** reply to that suggestion.

The defendant should also enclose copies of any documents the claimant asked for and also any documents relied upon in support of the defence.

 If the defendant makes it clear that the claim is contested, the claimant can start court proceedings. However, the idea is that by this time everybody should know where they stand.

If you claim is not covered by a pre-action protocol

Although there may be no formal procedure in other types of civil claim, pretty much the same rules apply. If you are a claimant, you or your solicitor should write a formal letter of claim making it clear why you say the defendant is liable. The fact that there is no pre-action protocol does not mean that you can go ahead and start the court action without giving the defendant any warning. You will be heavily criticised by the court if you do so. Likewise, if you are a defendant, you will need to send a formal reply setting out chapter and verse as to what your position is and, if you deny the allegations, why.

IF LIABILITY IS ADMITTED

If you are a claimant and the formal letter of response has come back with an admission that the defendant is liable, you ought to be able to breathe a sigh of relief and get on with the business of sorting out how much the defendant is going to pay you.

In most cases that is what happens, but sometimes it doesn't work out like that. Things can go wrong if the admission was made by someone who wasn't properly qualified to decide whether or not the defendant was liable. Eventually, the file will end up on the desk of someone more senior who may decide that, in fact, there is a good defence to the claim and this will result in the defendant trying to withdraw the admission.

In order to do this, the defendant will have to ask the court to allow the admission to be withdrawn. If there was a genuine mistake and no suggestion of any deliberate attempt to lull the claimant into a false sense of security, the court will almost certainly give permission for the admission to be withdrawn and the claim will then continue, to trial if necessary, just as if the admission had never been made.

Case Study — Mrs Turton

Mrs Turton's husband was killed in a car accident when a bullock escaped from a field and strayed on to the road. She wanted to claim damages from the bullock's owner who passed the claim to his insurers to deal with. Before proceedings started, the insurers admitted liability on behalf of the defendant. However, when the file was passed by the insurers to the solicitors, the admission was withdrawn and the defence denied liability.

The court decided that the admission was a result of the insurers' misunderstanding of the law and allowed the admission to be withdrawn. This was despite the fact that because of the admission, Mrs Turton's solicitor had not thought it necessary to investigate the circumstances of the accident or take statements from witnesses, and that Mrs Turton had already bought a bungalow on the strength of her belief that she would be receiving a large sum of damages.

Turton v Hellier (1 August 2005) Yeovil County Court

Starting proceedings

If you have a solicitor, he or she will issue proceedings on your behalf. Your involvement will probably be limited to checking and signing the particulars of claim (see pages 70-7), which has to be submitted with the claim form.

If you are dealing with the claim yourself and you cannot use the online service (see box on page 64), you will need to:

- **Complete a hard copy of the claim form N1.** These are available from your local court office or the Minstry of Justice website. Go to the home page on www.justice.gov.uk and click on 'What we do'. This will take you to a site index. Click on 'civil procedure rules' and choose 'forms' from the top menu.
- **Prepare your particulars of claim** (see pages 70–7).
- **Send or take three copies** each of form N1 and the particulars of claim to the court office.
- **Pay the court fee** (see opposite).

The court will process the paperwork and, unless you want to do so, will send the claim form to the defendant at the address you have provided.

The proceedings can be issued in whatever court you or your solicitor find

 Whatever the value of the claim, the procedure for issuing court proceedings is exactly the same. It is only after a defence has been filed that the case will be allocated to a track.

most convenient – regardless of where the incident leading to the claim took place. In fact, you have pretty much a free choice as to which court to issue proceedings in. The exceptions are:

- **Personal injury claims worth less than** £50,000 and all other claims (except defamation) worth less than £15,000, which must be started in the County Court.
- **Defamation claims,** which must be started in the High Court unless the defendant has given written agreement

 For the Civil Procedure Rules relating to starting proceedings, see CPR Part 7. If you are doing the claim yourself, you can find the nearest County Court on the court service website, which includes addresses and photographs of the courts. Go to: www.hmcourts-service.gov.uk.

for the claim to be issued in the County Court.

- **Claims for possession of property,** which should be started in the area where the property is situated.

NOTE Once the claim has been issued, the court will assign it a reference number. You should quote this in any correspondence you have with the court.

Court fees

These need to be paid at the time the claim or application is lodged.

What do you pay for?	How much?	Who pays?
Starting a claim worth up to £300	£30	Claimant
Starting a claim worth up to £500	£50	Claimant
Starting a claim worth up to £1,000	£80	Claimant
Starting a claim worth up to £5,000	£120	Claimant
Starting a claim worth up to £15,000	£250	Claimant
Starting a claim worth up to £50,000	£400	Claimant
Maximum court fee for starting a claim worth over £300,000 or of unlimited value	£1,700	Claimant
Filing the allocation questionnaires in a claim worth more than £1,500	£100	Claimant
Making an application during the proceedings	£65	Claimant or defendant, depending on whose application it is
Trial fee	Fast track: £275 Multi track: £500	Claimant, when the listing questionnaires (see page 153) are filed
Appeal	Small claims track: £100 All other claims: £120	Claimant or defendant, depending on whose appeal it is

Exemptions If you are or your partner are receiving certain benefits, including Income Support, Job Seeker's Allowance, Pension Credit, Working Tax Credit and Child Tax Credit, you are exempt from paying court fees. You can get further details from the Court Service website or the court.

Remission If you do not automatically qualify for an exemption but paying court fees would cause you financial hardship, you can apply for remission of the fees, which means that the cost will be waived or refunded to you. The application form is available on the Court Service website or from the court.

Using the internet

- A money claim for less than £100,000 can now be issued through the court service website. The claimant completes the claim form and pays the court fee online. The court then prints it off and sends it to the defendant, who can respond by post in the normal way or online.

- A claim for possession of rented or mortgaged residential property can also be issued online in the same way as a money claim. The claim will automatically be logged in to the correct County Court for the location of the property.

Go to www.hmcourts-service.gov.uk and click on 'Online services' where there is information on using HMCS money and possession claims online.

Once the claim has been started online it is possible for both parties to track its progress on the court service website.

There is also a pilot scheme involving nine County Courts allowing a number of other court forms to be completed and lodged online. Details of the courts involved and the forms available can be found on the website: www.hmcourts-service.gov.uk. Go on to the website and click 'forms', which provides a quick link to the pilot scheme. Click 'user guide' and go to 'courts' and then click on 'pilot courts' to find out if your local court is included in the pilot scheme.

" A claim that is issued online can subsequently be tracked by both parties to assess its progress. "

Note

You cannot issue your claim online if:

- You are receiving legal aid.
- Either the claimant or defendant is a child or an adult who lacks mental capacity.
- Your claim is against the Crown.
- You are a 'vexatious litigant' who has been forbidden by the court from taking part in any more civil claims (you will know if this applies to you).

BRINGING A CLAIM ON BEHALF OF SOMEONE ELSE

There are always instances when a person cannot bring their own claim.

On behalf of a child

A child below the age of 18 will need a **litigation friend** to bring or defend the claim on his or her behalf: usually a parent – although any responsible adult who is willing can act as a litigation friend. If a settlement is agreed, it must be approved by the court and any damages awarded to the child are paid into an account held by the court. The money can only be withdrawn when the child reaches the age of 18 (although it is possible to apply to the court before then for permission to withdraw enough to pay for something specific that the child needs, such as a computer).

In order to approve a settlement, the judge will want to see a written advice from a barrister specialising in that type of claim confirming that the agreement is in the child's interest. The court will almost certainly refuse to approve anything unless the child has had proper legal representation.

❝ The money can only be withdrawn when the child reaches the age of 18 years. ❞

Involving an adult who is a 'patient'

Similar rules apply if one of the parties to the claim is a 'patient'; that is, someone who, because of a learning disability or their state of health, lacks the mental capacity to deal with court proceedings or make informed decisions. However, in cases where there is no realistic prospect of the disability coming to an end, a receiver may be appointed to administer the finances and if there is a large sum of money involved, a trust will usually be set up to ensure that the patient's interests are looked after.

Where someone has died

Even after someone has died, their estate may make or receive a claim and those who are responsible for dealing with the estate must pursue or defend the claim on its behalf. This will be the executors, if there was a will, or whoever has been appointed to administer the estate (usually the widow or close family member) if the person concerned died intestate.

If you are bringing a claim against the estate of someone who has died and the paperwork has not yet been sorted out, you can start your claim against 'The Personal Representatives of John Brown deceased' and then ask the court to appoint someone to represent the estate.

 For the Civil Procedure Rules relating to bringing a claim on behalf of someone else, see CPR Part 21 (on behalf of a child or involving an adult who is a 'patient') and CPR Part 19.8 (where someone has died).

WHAT TO DO IF YOU RECEIVE A CLAIM

Even if you have had plenty of warning that the claimant is going to take you to court, the arrival of formal court documents can be a shock. If you haven't already done so, you must consider getting legal advice. If you want to deal with it yourself, you will find the options set out on the claim form. They are:

1   Admit the whole claim.
2   Admit part of the claim and deny part of the claim.
3   Deny the whole claim.

One of the documents included with the claim form is an **acknowledgement of service**, which should be returned to the court within 14 days. It's a good idea to send it even if you intend to admit the whole claim. It will buy you some time to try and agree with the claimant that you will pay the money claimed and any costs the claimant is entitled to (just the court fee if the claim is for less than £5,000) without having a judgment entered against you. Once the payment has been made, you and the claimant simply tell the court the case has been settled (see pages 110–15 for the procedure).

If you do nothing at all, the claimant will be able to ask the court for judgment to be entered against you after the deadline for serving the acknowledgement of service or your defence expires.

Jargon buster

Acknowledgement of Service Form completed by the defendant confirming the claim form has been received

> **“ Even if you have had warning that the claimant is taking you to court, the arrival of formal documents can be a shock. Consider getting legal advice. ”**

 For the Civil Procedure Rules relating to what to do if you receive a claim, see CPR Parts 9, 10, 14, 15 and 16.

THE IMPORTANCE OF TIME LIMITS

At every stage of the court proceedings, deadlines are set. Missing a deadline can cause all sorts of problems and, in an extreme case, can mean that you cannot use a particular piece of evidence or even that your case is struck out. The court rules set out how time is calculated:

- **The date the claim is issued** is the day when the claim form was received by the court office and not the day on which it was entered on the court records or sent out. It is important to be aware of this as certain time limits (see the table on page 68) are laid down by the courts.
- **Where a claim form is sent out by first class post** the date of service (the date on which the defendant is taken to have received it) is two days after it was posted. The same rule applies to all court documents, including the defence and also documents sent by email.
- **Where the court allows a number of days to do something,** it means 'clear days'. For example, if the claim form arrives on 1 October, the last day for the acknowledgement of service to be received is 16 October.

- If **five days or less is allowed by the court to do something,** weekends and bank holidays are not counted.

 When you post a letter or court document, you don't need to send it by registered or recorded delivery. First class post is fine; but always make sure you get a certificate of posting.

" The date the claim is issued is the day when the claim form was received by the court office and not the day on which it was entered on the court records. "

 For the Civil Procedure Rules relating to the importance of time limits, see CPR Parts 2.8 and 6.7.

Time limits

These are the time limits the parties must work to in order to get the claim up and running.

Claimant	Defendant
Has four months from the date the claim form was received by the court to get it to the defendant	Has 14 days from receiving the claim form to get the acknowledgement of service back to the court
If the particulars of claim was not attached to the claim form, the claimant has 14 days from the day the claim form was sent to the defendant to forward the particulars of claim (see page 000) to him or her	Has 14 days after the acknowledgement of service is sent to prepare and send the defence Or Has 14 days after the particulars of claim (see page 70) arrives to return a defence
On receiving a defence and counterclaim, the claimant must prepare and send to the defendant a defence to the counterclaim within 14 days	If the defendant wants to make a claim against the claimant arising out of the same facts, the counterclaim should be included with the defence and sent at the same time

Note The parties can, if they want to, agree to allow each other more time to complete the various stages above. If agreement cannot be reached and one side really does need more time, they can ask the court to extend the deadline, but they will need a good reason for requiring extra time.

66 Time limits must be adhered to – they are not there just for the sake of it. 99

COUNTERCLAIMS

A counterclaim is a claim brought by the defendant against the claimant in the same proceedings. If, for example, you are being sued for not paying for goods that you say were faulty, you will want the court to make a finding about the faulty goods and how that affects your liability to pay for them. The counterclaim is usually prepared and sent out at the same time as the defence.

THIRD PARTY CLAIMS

The defendant may want to blame somebody else for what happened and bring him or her into the court proceedings (known as making a Part 20 claim). Someone brought into the proceedings in this way is known as a Third Party (if more than one person is involved, there may be Fourth, Fifth and Sixth parties, etc.). The defendant will need to complete an N211 claim form, which can either be obtained from the court or downloaded from the Ministry of Justice website (www.justice. gov.uk). You can also obtain guidance notes from the website which tell you what to do if you are a defendant making a Part 20 claim (N211A) or a Third Party (N211C).

As long as the Part 20 claim is issued at the same time as the defence is filed, the defendant does not need to get permission from the court to do this. The Part 20 claim form is then sent to the Third Party, and unless they admit liability, they must also prepare and file a defence.

❝ A counterclaim is brought by the defendant against the claimant. It is usually prepared and sent out at the same time as the defence. ❞

 For the Civil Procedure Rules relating to counterclaims and Third Party claims, see CPR Part 20.

69

Statements of case

Statements of case are the formal documents in which each side sets out its case. This enables the court to see what each party is saying about the claim and where the disagreement lies. For fast and multi track cases it is usual for a barrister to draft statements of case, which are also referred to as pleadings.

THE CLAIMANT'S STATEMENT OF CASE

The claimant's statement of case is known as the **particulars of claim.** The information is usually arranged in numbered paragraphs and should include:

- A summary of the facts, including the relationship between the claimant and defendant.
- Specific allegations of wrongdoing against the defendant (including the date on which they occurred).
- A brief summary of the effect of the defendant's wrongdoing on the claimant or of any financial loss caused.
- If damages are claimed, a claim for interest to be paid on the damages.
- Details of the remedy the claimant wants. If specific sums of money, or special damages, are claimed, the particulars of claim should say what they are for. If **general damages** are claimed for the effect the defendant's wrongdoing has had on the claimant, a brief description of what the claimant has suffered should be included.

" The particulars of claim include a summary of the facts, specific allegations and details of the remedy that the claimant wants. "

 For the Civil Procedure Rules relating to statement of case, see CPR Part 16.

Particulars of claim – special requirements

Type of claim	Special requirements
Building or housing disrepair claims	If there is a long list of faults or things that need repair, it is good practice to set them out in a separate schedule, which can be attached to the particulars of claim
Contract disputes	A copy of the contract should be attached. If there is no written agreement, the words used to make the agreement must be set out as fully as possible
Fraud	Allegations of fraud should not be made lightly. If fraud is to be alleged, all the facts that give rise to the allegation must be set out in full
Human rights	You must give precise details of the European Convention right that you say has been breached and what remedy you want. This is a specialist area of law and unless you have had legal advice that there has been a breach, it is unlikely that you will be able to use a human rights argument. Don't be tempted to make a general assertion that the defendant's conduct has breached your human rights. The court won't be impressed
Personal injury and clinical negligence claims	Must include: • Claimant's date of birth • Description of injury Attachments: • A schedule of all the financial expenses and losses claimed • Medical report describing the injury

Jargon buster

Case management The way in which the court controls the progress of the claim up to trial

Claim form The court form you or your solicitor need to complete to start the claim

Directions Orders made by the court for the things that need to be done to get the claim ready for trial

Issue (proceedings or an application) To start in the court

Letter of claim A letter that puts the defendant on notice that the claimant intends to take court action

Reply Document in which the claimant specifically responds to the defence. Only really necessary in very complicated cases or where the defence raises a completely new argument

Service/serve Ensuring that the formal court papers are received by other parties to the claim

Stay in proceedings Putting the claim on hold – usually to allow settlement negotiations to take place

To file or lodge a document To send or give it to the court

THE DEFENDANT'S STATEMENT OF CASE

The defendant's statement of case is known as the **defence**. In the defence, each fact, allegation and demand contained in the particulars of claim must either be admitted or denied or neither admitted nor denied (this is where the defendant simply is not in a position to say one way or another). Where the particulars of claim has numbered paragraphs it makes it easy for the defence to go through, dealing with each one in turn.

❝ A useful way to summarise facts for the defence is to set them out in bullet points. ❞

Types of damages

Aggravated damages Only available in certain cases, such as assault or wrongful imprisonment. Extra compensation when the circumstances of the case mean that the effect of the wrong doing was to cause particular distress to the claimant

Exemplary damages Only available in certain cases, such as unlawful eviction. They are designed to penalise a defendant where the motive for the wrongdoing was financial gain

Extra compensation When the circumstances of the case mean that the effect of the wrongdoing was to cause particular distress to the claimant

General damages Damages that cannot be precisely calculated. They compensate for the effect of the defendant's wrongdoing – such as physical or mental injury or emotional upset

Provisional damages If there is a recognised risk of a medical condition developing later on in a personal injury claim, and it does, in fact, develop, the claimant can come back to court to claim more damages

Special damages Expenses and financial losses, such as the cost of repairs or replacement, loss of earnings, etc.

Unliquidated damages Still to be quantified

PREPARING YOUR STATEMENT OF CASE

If you are doing your own particulars of claim or defence, you can use the space on the form provided if what you want to say is relatively short. Otherwise you should set the whole thing out on a separate sheet of paper. You will obviously need to spend a little time working out how to put your case. It's a good idea to prepare a draft before you write up the final version.

Summarise the facts

If you are the claimant, start by setting out in bullet points the facts that you think are important, keeping your summary short and simple. Remember that the statement of case is not the same as a witness statement. You don't have to explain absolutely everything that happened or go into a lot of detail about what was said at the time. In most cases, you should be able to summarise the facts in no more than five bullet points, and it can often be done in much less.

If you are the defendant and you agree with the facts in the particulars of claim, you can simply admit them. If you have a different version, you should deny them and set out your own account of what happened.

Liability

If you are the claimant, set out again in bullet points the reasons why you say the defendant is at fault.

If you are the defendant, go through each allegation the claimant has made against you. Decide first whether you admit it, deny it or neither admit nor deny it.

If you are admitting or neither admitting nor denying, that is really all you have to say in answer to the allegation.

If you are denying a specific allegation, you should try to give the reason why you deny it (it may be obvious if your version of the facts is very different from the claimant's).

66 When summarising the facts, you don't have to explain everything that happened at the time in great detail. 99

The remedy

If you are the claimant, think about what you want the court to do and try to give a realistic value to the claim. Do not ask for an unlimited or enormous amount of damages just on the off chance. If you are claiming damages, you should also ask for interest.

If you are the defendant, do not simply deny that the claimant is entitled to anything. The better tactic is usually to 'put the claimant to strict proof' that he or she is entitled to the remedy they are asking for. This means that the claimant has to produce evidence in order to show that they really are entitled to the remedy they are asking for. You can, however, challenge specific facts that the claimant relies on to support the request for a remedy.

Double-check everything

Now go back through all the bullet points you have made and see how they read. Delete any points that repeat something said before and be fairly brutal in editing out unnecessary detail that can be used later on in your witness statement (see page 125). Now go through and number your bullet points and you should have a working statement of case.

❝ It is vital that you check that every detail in your statement of truth is accurate. ❞

Claiming interest

The courts have the power to make the defendant pay interest on any damages that are awarded. The County Court has this power under section 69 of the County Courts Act 1984 and the High Court gets it from s31A of the Supreme Court Act 1981. The judge takes the final decision about how much interest, if any, should be paid. The normal rule is that interest on financial losses runs from the date of loss or expenditure at the 'special account rate', which is currently 6 per cent (2007). Interest on general damages for injury or upset is currently 2 per cent (2007) from the date on which the court proceedings were started.

Statement of truth

Whether you are doing the claim yourself or you have a solicitor, you will need to sign a statement confirming the truth of your statement of case. (If you are legally represented, your solicitor can do it on your behalf if time is short.) It is vital that you check that every detail in your statement of case is accurate. Don't assume that because it has been prepared by a lawyer it must be right.

If you prepared it yourself, make sure that all the dates are correct and make it clear if there's anything you're not completely sure about by using such phrases as, 'The claimant believes that', 'To the best of the defendant's knowledge' or 'On or around 21 March'. (See CPR Part 22 for the Civil Procedure Rules.)

Ask the expert

I am a kitchen fitter. I'm being sued by a couple I installed a kitchen for. They were always difficult clients and before I had a chance to come back to do the snagging, they had sent a letter of claim. The main thing that they're complaining about is damp rising up the back wall but that's not down to me – it is simply that when I stripped out the room the problem became obvious. However, there are a few things that did need to be sorted out and if they had given me the chance, I would have done them. My solicitor has tried negotiating with theirs. In fact, because I just wanted it sorted, we put forward a without prejudice offer of £4,500, which is much more than the cost of the outstanding work. Needless to say, they turned it down and now it looks like we're going to court. The letter of response that my solicitor wrote admits that some of the complaints (i.e. those relating to jobs on the snagging list) are justified. I'm not happy about this. I think for tactical reasons we should simply have denied everything. Also I'm worried that if the judge gets wind of the fact that we offered as much as £4,500, he'll think there must be some truth in their allegations.

Since you accept that there were things that needed to be done, your solicitor really had no choice but to admit them. If you had written the letter of response, you would have had to have done the same. In fact, it seems as if you have a good argument as to why you didn't complete the jobs on the snagging list, so the fact that you have admitted from the beginning that there were a few things still to be seen to should, if anything, help your case if the claim goes to trial.

The trial judge will not be aware of the offer of £4,500 that you made but will approach the claim without preconceptions either way. In the meantime, your solicitor should be able to advise as to what steps you can now take to protect your position (see pages 110–15).

Examples of a Particulars of Claim and Defence

The following four pages contain examples of how to set out your statement of case for the court. The particulars of claim are prepared by the claimant and the defence by the defendant.

IN THE NORWICH COUNTY COURT

BETWEEN

RAYMOND HARRIS

Claimant

and

MICHAEL ROWNTREE

Defendant

PARTICULARS OF CLAIM

1. The claimant lives at 44 Pickering Lane, Norwich.

2. Since June 2005 the defendant has lived in the house next door at 46 Pickering Lane.

3. From the time the defendant moved in to 46 Pickering Lane he has caused a nuisance to the claimant:

PARTICULARS OF NUISANCE

1. Playing loud rock music at all hours of the day and night. The most recent occasions when this occurred were: June 24th, June 29th, July 7th and July 16th 2007.
2. Banging on the walls and using a drill for hours on end. This happened every day between June 30th and July 24th.
3. Dumping building materials, including old bricks and rubble, in the claimant's front garden.
4. Large numbers of the defendant's friends regularly congregate in the defendant's back garden. They are noisy and often drunk and on one occasion one of them vomited over the fence into the claimant's garden.

4. On many occasions the claimant has asked the defendant not to behave in this manner and to remove the rubbish from the claimant's front garden but the defendant has failed to take any notice of these requests.

5. The defendant's conduct has caused the claimant upset and inconvenience and financial loss:

PARTICULARS OF INCONVENIENCE AND UPSET

The claimant often works night shifts and the defendant's activities have often disrupted his sleep. Sometimes the noise coming from next door is so loud that it stops the claimant from listening to the radio or watching television. Since the problems started he has felt unable to invite friends or family to the house, which is very upsetting.

PARTICULARS OF DAMAGE

The cost of removing the building materials and rubble from the claimant's front garden £164.88
On two occasions the claimant overslept after sleepless nights and lost earnings of £489.00

6. The claimant is entitled to be paid interest on any money awarded by the court under the provisions of the County Courts Act 1984.

AND the claimant is seeking:
1. An order forbidding the defendant from behaving in a way which causes a nuisance to the claimant
2. Damages of not more than £5,000
3. Interest

The claimant believes that the facts set out in the above particulars of claim are true.
Signed

DATED 28th AUGUST 2007

IN THE NORWICH COUNTY COURT
BETWEEN

RAYMOND HARRIS

<u>Claimant</u>

and

MICHAEL ROWNTREE

<u>Defendant</u>

<u>DEFENCE</u>

1. The defendant admits paragraphs 1 and 2 of the Particulars of Claim.

2. As for paragraph 3, the defendant denies that he has ever behaved in a way that would cause the claimant a nuisance and says in particular that:

    1. He does not own a sound system. He has a radio which he sometimes listens to rock music on, but never has it turned up loud enough to cause the claimant a nuisance.
    2. The defendant admits that during the first three weeks of April he had builders in the house. He warned the claimant and anyway most of the work took place while the claimant was at work. The claimant did not complain at the time. If he had done so, the defendant would have sorted it out.
    3. The defendant admits that the builders inadvertently dumped some empty cement bags on the claimant's side of the communal front garden. When the claimant pointed this out to the defendant he moved them immediately. The bricks, rubble and other building materials were left on the defendant's side of the front garden.

4. The defendant admits that sometimes he has friends round. He denies that they get excessively noisy or drunk. The defendant neither admits nor denies the allegation that one of his friends was sick into the claimant's garden. He says that if it did happen it was without his knowledge or authority so he cannot be held responsible for it.

3. As for paragraph 4, the defendant admits that there have been a number of arguments between himself and the claimant in which the claimant has been abusive and threatening. He denies that the claimant asked him to stop causing a nuisance and/or to remove the building materials from the garden. The claimant's main concern was the defendant's relationship with his daughter.

4. The financial loss claimed by the claimant is denied. The claimant had the building materials removed from the defendant's side of the front garden without permission when in fact the defendant was intending to reuse the bricks.

5. Further the claimant has been heard to boast that he has never missed a day's work in 34 years and is put to strict proof of the loss of earnings he claims. The inconvenience and upset are also denied.

6. The claim for interest is neither admitted nor denied.

The defendant believes that the facts set out in this Defence are true.
Signed

DATED SEPTEMBER 19th 2007

JUDGMENT IN DEFAULT

If the defendant does not return either the acknowledgement of service or lodge a defence in the time allowed, the claimant can ask the court to enter judgment in default (of a defence). If the claim is for a set amount of money, the claimant can immediately take steps to enforce the judgment and make the defendant pay.

If the claim includes **unliquidated damages** (where the amount of damages needs to be decided by the court – for example, general damages for an injury), the court will arrange a short **disposal hearing** to decide how much the claimant is entitled to.

The defendant can apply to the court to have a judgment in default **set aside**. If a defence was not served because the defendant had not received the court papers or because the claim had already been paid in full, the judgment will always be set aside. Otherwise, the defendant will have to show that there is a real chance of successfully defending the claim. The defendant will also have to explain why the deadline was missed and the court will specifically look at how quickly the defendant acted to try and sort things out once the deadline had passed.

Jargon buster

Consent order An order made by the court that everyone agrees to

Disposal hearing Hearing to decide the amount of damages the defendant must pay after judgment in default has been entered against him or her

Judgment in default Judgment given because the defendant has not filed the acknowledgement of service or a defence

Set aside (an order) Cancel so that to all intents and purposes it was never made

Allocating the case to a track

Once the defence has been lodged with the court, the court will send out allocation questionnaires to all the parties. The purpose of the questionnaire is to help the district judge, who first looks at the case, decide which track the case should be allocated to.

The allocation questionnaire is designed to give the court an idea of where the case has got to. Each side must say how many witnesses they want to call, whether experts will be needed and how much they estimate their costs for the claim are going to be. They also have to say whether they have followed any pre-action protocol that applied to the claim and whether they would like the court to give them an opportunity to try to negotiate a settlement. The court is supposed to send a copy of your opponent's questionnaire to you or your solicitor, but doesn't always do so. If you don't receive a copy from the court, it is worth arranging to exchange questionnaires directly with your opponent so that you can see how they assess the complexity of the case at this relatively early stage.

CHANGING TRACK

The court rules say that the value of the claim will normally decide which track the claim goes on to; but either the claimant or the defendant can ask for it to go on a different track (either on the allocation questionnaire or, if that doesn't work, by making an application to the court). In either case, the court will want to know the reason for requesting another track. For more information on changing track and the cost implications, see page 104.

❝ Seeing your opponent's allocation questionnaire will show you how they assess the complexity of the claim. ❞

For the Civil Procedure Rules relating to allocating the case to a track, see CPR Part 26. Part 26.8 explains the rules for changing track.

Still time to talk

The fact that the claimant has taken the serious step of issuing court proceedings does not mean that the claim will now inevitably go to trial. This should be obvious from the fact that the allocation questionnaire gives the parties another opportunity to opt for a stay in the proceedings for a set period of time so that they can try to reach an agreement. If both sides are willing to have a go at sorting out the claim, the court will be only too happy to agree to a stay and will not allocate the case to a track. Any other deadlines that were coming up can be ignored for the time being and each side should avoid doing anything that adds to the cost of the claim, such as arranging for an expert report.

If it's possible to come to an agreement, a consent order can be drawn up that both sides are happy with, which is then sent to the court for its approval – which it almost certainly will get. If there is no settlement by the end of the time allowed, the file will go back to a district judge who will allocate the case and decide whether anything else needs to be done. The proceedings then continue as if they had never stopped and what happens next will depend on which track the case has been allocated to.

❝Even after court proceedings have been issued, the claim need not necessarily go to trial – an agreement can still be settled out of court.❞

The three approaches to civil claims

This section looks at the differences between the ways claims are dealt with on each of the three tracks. The main emphasis is on the small claims track for the simple reason that if your case is a fast track or a multi track claim, it is likely that you will have a solicitor who will deal with all the procedural stages of the claim for you and a barrister to present your case at trial.

4

Small claims track

If your claim has been allocated to the small claims track there will be nothing unusual about the fact that you are doing the case yourself. That is precisely what the court expects to happen and because of that, the process is designed to be as user-friendly as possible.

THE SMALL CLAIMS TRACK IN A NUTSHELL

The small claims track is designed for claims worth less than £5,000. It has a simplified procedure (CPR Part 27), which should mean that claims are dealt with more quickly than on the other tracks.

There are some key similarities between the small claims track and the fast and multi tracks:

- **The procedure for starting the claim** in the court is the same (see page 62).
- **The claim will be transferred** to the defendant's local court (see page 104).
- **If you think your opponent** does not stand a chance of winning, you can apply for summary judgment (see page 151).
- **The court** can decide that expert evidence on a particular point should be given by a jointly instructed expert (see page 131).

- **The hearing is public;** anyone can sit in on it.
- **The hearing is recorded.**
- **The judge must give reasons** for his or her decision.
- **The loser can appeal** against the decision (see pages 182–91).

And there are also some key differences:

- **Costs awarded** are limited to the court fee, witness expenses and expert evidence, unless there has been 'unreasonable conduct' (see box on page 96 and the case study on page 97).
- **If you don't want to do the case yourself,** you can have anyone you like to represent you, including someone who has no legal experience or training.
- **The hearing is less formal.** It will usually take place in the judge's office, not a courtroom. It is not necessary to take the oath and there are no

 For information about fast track claims and the differences between the fast track and the small claims track, see pages 99-100.

restrictions about how the evidence is given. The district judge will decide how the hearing should be run.

- **It is possible for you to put your case in writing** instead of coming to the hearing.
- **If both sides agree,** the district judge can decide the case by reading all the documents instead of having a hearing.
- **If one of the parties does not attend the hearing** for a 'good' reason, they can ask the court to set aside the decision and have a rehearing.
- **You cannot get legal aid** for a small claims track case.
- **Apart from an injunction,** you cannot apply for any of the other interim remedies available on the fast or multi track.
- **The formal rules of evidence and disclosure** of documents do not apply.

Once the case has been allocated, the court file will go to a district judge to decide what directions need to be given to get the case ready for hearing. The directions are set out in a court order and sent to both parties. In a very straightforward claim they can be limited to a requirement that before the hearing each side should provide copies of any documents that they want to use to support their case and that they bring the originals to court. For particular types of case, the directions are more specific

about the types of documents the court will want to see (see table on page 86).

The fact that the directions include a request for any expert evidence to be produced, does not mean that there is any obligation on either side to get such evidence. In fact, before you get expert evidence, you must get permission from the court to do so. The court will only allow you to use an expert if it's necessary to decide the claim, so if you do want to ask for permission, you should be able to identify the area of dispute that you say the expert evidence will help to resolve. If you win, you can claim for the cost of getting an expert's report, but there is an upper limit of £200.

If either of the statements of case is confusing or difficult to understand, the district judge can include an order for the party concerned to clarify their case. The order will usually make it clear how this is to be done. For example, by giving details of damage suffered or listing the faults in goods that were supplied.

❝ If you think you need evidence from an expert, you must get permission from the court. If you win, you can claim up to £200 of the cost of this. ❞

For information about multi track claims and the differences between the multi track and the small claims track, see pages 101-2.

Document checklist for different types of claim

Type of claim	Documents required
Claims involving rented property, such as housing disrepair or return of the deposit	✓ Tenancy agreement ✓ Rent book or other proof of payment of rent ✓ Witness statements ✓ Photographs ✓ Estimates or invoices for repair work
Contractual dispute (e.g. building work, car repairs, etc.)	✓ Copy of the contract, if there is one ✓ Photographs ✓ Witness statements ✓ Invoices or estimates for repairs/ making good ✓ Experts' reports (if there are any)
Holiday and wedding claims	✓ Brochure ✓ Booking form or contract ✓ Proof of payment ✓ Photographs ✓ Witness statements ✓ Letters
Road accident	✓ Sketch plan and photographs ✓ Witness statements ✓ Any expert reports – including a medical report if someone was injured ✓ Invoices and estimates for repairs and documents relating to any other losses claimed, such as loss of earnings

❝ You and your opponent will need to provide witness statements, so you will see all the evidence in advance. This includes your own statement. ❞

PREPARING YOUR WITNESS STATEMENTS

In most claims, the court will ask you to provide witness statements so that both the judge and your opponent know in advance what your evidence is going to be. Since your opponent will have to do the same thing, you should also have a good idea of what his or her evidence is going to be in time for the hearing.

Don't forget that you need to prepare a witness statement of your own evidence as well as for anyone else who will be giving evidence on your behalf.

The best place to start is by looking at the particulars of claim and the defence. Your statement of case contains the bare outline of your claim. Now you need to put the flesh on the bones. Your opponent's statement of case should set out the facts that support his or her case and which, as far as possible, you must deal with in your evidence.

- **Make a list of everything that happened,** including conversations, letters, etc., setting it all out in chronological order.
- **Check your list against the statements of case,** making sure that everything is covered and that you have not included anything that is not directly relevant to the claim. Then you can fill in the detail of the events that you need to describe.
- **Do not ignore documents or facts** that you think may be unhelpful to your case. You can be absolutely certain that if you don't put them in, you will have to answer questions about them at the hearing and it is much

better to try to deal with them when you are not under the immediate pressure of cross-examination or questions from the judge. If there have been occasions when you have acted in the heat of the moment, it is much better to acknowledge what happened, and, if possible, provide an explanation:

'I know it was stupid of me to lose my temper when I telephoned the defendant, but I really was so angry about the state he had left the kitchen in and the fact that he was refusing to reply to my letters and messages.'

❝ Keep the witness statement as short and simple as possible – you need to keep the judge's attention so that he or she can absorb the salient facts with ease. ❞

Although it is important not to miss anything out that is relevant to the claim, try to keep your witness statement as short and simple as possible. The most important person who will be reading it is the judge and you want to keep his or her attention all the way through, which may be difficult if the statement gets bogged down in a lot of detail about things that are not really relevant to the matters in dispute.

Observing the formalities

As the strict rules of evidence do not apply to the small claims track, no one is going to criticise you if you produce witness statements that are not set out in the way the court usually requires. However, since the purpose of the rules is to make witness statements easier to use and to ensure that the evidence they contain is as helpful and clearly presented as possible, you may want to set out your statement in the format that is described here:

- **Name and address** This may sound obvious, but you should set out at the beginning the name and address of the person making the statement, and, if relevant, who they are:

    'I am Victoria Parker of 97 Broad Street, London W15 XYT and I am the claimant's sister.'

- **Numbered paragraphs and pages** As with your statement of case, your witness statements should be set out in numbered paragraphs. It is also a good idea to number the pages.

Exhibits

If you want to refer to documents or photographs, it is good practice to attach copies of them to your statement and to give each one a reference number so that everybody knows which document is being referred to. Documents and photographs attached to a witness statement are usually referred to as exhibits. Documents should be given a reference number based on your initials and in the order in which they are exhibited to your statement. So if your name is Peter Brown, the first letter or document you exhibit to your statement will be PB.1. You should make sure that each document is referred to and identified in your statement. For example:

'I wrote a letter to the claimant on 24 March 2007 (see exhibit PB.2) in which I told him that I did not accept the faults he was complaining about were my responsibility. He did not reply until 28 April 2007 (see exhibit PB.3) and seemed to ignore completely what I had said.'

If you are preparing statements for other witnesses, you will use their initials and not yours to exhibit documents to their statements.

 The examples of a Particulars of Claim and Defence on pages 76-9 will give you an idea as to how to number paragraphs and lay out the information.

Photographs can simply be numbered, but again it is usual to give them an overall reference number and to say when and by whom they were taken. It is also helpful to prepare a key explaining what each photograph shows, which is placed with the photographs.

'I went back to the scene of the accident the next day with my brother and he took a number of photographs (see exhibit SL.4), which give an idea of what traffic conditions were like at the time of the accident.'

Jargon buster

Disallow costs To refuse to make an order that the other party should pay the amount and/or the costs claimed

Exhibit A document or photograph that forms part of the evidence of a witness and is attached to their statement

Listing a case or application Setting the date for the hearing

Statement of truth

The evidence in your witness statement will have added force if you finish it with a statement of truth:

'I believe the contents of the above statement are true.'

Signed and dated

At the end of the statement, after the statement of truth, the maker of the statement should sign and date it.

❝ Documents (known as exhibits) should be given a reference number based on your initials, in the order they appear in your statement. ❞

PREPARING FOR THE HEARING

The court will notify you when the hearing is going to take place and apart from ensuring that you know where the court is, you should also spend some time preparing your case for the hearing.

Organising the paperwork

The first thing you must do is organise the papers so that you are able to locate any document easily and quickly. The best way of doing this is to arrange all the papers in a ring folder. You can adopt your own system but it probably makes sense to order them as follows:

- First, the claim form and particulars of claim.
- Then the defence.
- The witness statements, first for the claimant, and then the defendant.
- Any documents, including correspondence, which you want to refer to as well as the documents your

opponent has sent to you and which are not exhibited to the witness statements.

- Finally, place any orders from the court at the back.

Make sure you keep copies of any letters or documents that you send to the court or your opponent.

Use markers to provide immediate access to the documents that are particularly important.

You should also have a few loose blank sheets of paper in the folder to make notes on during the hearing.

If you have sent any documents through to the court within a week or so of the hearing, it is sensible to take along spare copies, just in case they didn't reach the court file before it went to the judge. If paperwork has gone astray, the easiest way to deal with this at the hearing is to hand the judge another copy.

If you haven't received any documents or witness statements from your opponent and the final hearing is only a couple of weeks away, you should write to him or her pointing this out and asking that anything that he or she wants to use at the hearing should be sent to you as a matter of urgency. Send a copy of your letter to the court with a covering note expressing your concern. Otherwise,

if your opponent turns up at court with documents you've never seen before, you may have to choose between trying to deal with the new material there and then or having the hearing adjourned.

If it's obvious that your opponent has ignored a specific request to provide documents, there is a good chance the judge won't allow him or her to use them and will go ahead with the hearing anyway. Even if the judge does allow them to be used, he or she is likely to be extremely critical of your opponent and this can only work in your favour.

Getting your case ready

Although the district judge can choose how the hearing is conducted, at some point you will be asked to explain your case and give your side of the story. You will also almost certainly have the opportunity to make some closing comments before the judge decides who has won. In addition, you can expect to be questioned both by the judge and your opponent and you will have the chance to ask your opponent questions – although you might find that the judge may cut short prolonged cross-examination by either side.

Evidence or argument?

It is important to remember the difference between evidence and argument.

- **Evidence** involves describing the facts.
- **Argument** is all about explaining why you should win the case.

In general terms, evidence is dealt with at the hearing through questions and answers. Argument is dealt with by giving each party the opportunity to comment upon the evidence and make any other points that help their case (see also the box, right).

Preparing the evidence

Make a note of any facts that both sides agree on. It is unusual to have a case where absolutely everything is disputed and there is nothing to be gained from spending a lot of time on evidence if it turns out there is actually no argument about it. It will help the judge to know what can be agreed and enable him or her to concentrate on the real areas of disagreement.

- Prepare the questions you want to put to your opponent and any witnesses who will give evidence in support of his or her case. You can use their witness statements as the basis for planning the questions you want to ask.
- Go through the witness statement(s) with a highlighter, marking up the important differences between their evidence and yours. You can then use

Spot the difference

Evidence
I was sitting in a queue of traffic in my car at the junction of Belsize Road and Clapton Street. It was rush hour and the traffic was very heavy so that even though the lights had turned green in my favour, nothing in front of me was moving when I suddenly felt the impact of the defendant's car running into the back of me. He says that I had started to move through the lights and then stopped suddenly for no reason. That's just not true. The way ahead of me was blocked by other vehicles.

Argument
It's simply not believable that I would have stopped for no reason while driving through traffic lights. It was obviously the defendant's fault; either he was going too fast or he wasn't paying attention to what was going on at the junction, or both. Anyway, even if I had stopped suddenly, he should have allowed enough space between our vehicles to stop safely.

that as the basis for deciding on the questions that you want to ask.

- Make a short list of what you think are the most important pieces of your evidence, so that you will have the core facts of your claim at your fingertips.

Place yourself in your opponent's position and go through your statement of case trying to look for any weak point and thinking about how you would deal with a question on it. However, don't spend too much time doing this. You should have confidence in your case. You need to strike a balance between being ready to explain any apparent weaknesses in your evidence and being too eager to make concessions.

Preparing the arguments

In a lot of claims, the facts will speak for themselves and you will not need to spend much time arguing your case in front of the judge.

- Try to keep the points you want to make as short and simple as possible. Once again, you need to hold the judge's attention and you are more likely to do this if you cut straight to the real points in dispute.
- Do not launch into a personal attack on your opponent. If he or she has behaved badly, the judge will almost certainly pick up this fact from the evidence presented.
- Summarise the arguments in favour of your case and your answer to the arguments of your opponent in a series of bullet points. If you can open your argument by saying to the judge

'There are three reasons why you should decide the claim in my favour', and then be able to go through each one, so much the better.

Do not be tempted to write a full-length speech. The way the evidence comes out at the hearing may give a very different slant to the case from the one that appears in the witness statements and you need to be able to deal with that on the day. Also the judge may decide that there are only one or two specific points the parties need to comment on. If you have gone to the hearing planning to deliver a speech you have written in advance, you may be completely thrown if you have to deal with a different way of presenting your argument. In any event, reading or reciting a speech prepared in advance is never a good way of putting forward a convincing argument. However nervous you feel, it is always better to be spontaneous in the way in which you present your case.

❝ Don't prepare a speech: the judge may only want you to comment on one or two specific points. ❞

 Chapter 6 looks at the different forms of evidence in more detail, starting on page 119.

CONTACT WITH YOUR OPPONENT

Keep it businesslike, short and to the point. If you speak on the telephone, it is sensible to make a note at the time of what was said (solicitors always do this). If anything important is discussed or agreed during a telephone call, write a letter to your opponent confirming what was said.

CONTACT WITH THE COURT

Most County Court staff are friendly and happy to answer any queries you may have. When you receive letters and court orders, make sure you read them carefully and if there is anything you don't understand, give the court a ring and ask. If you know you are going to have problems meeting a time limit, write at once to the court giving the reason why you can't meet the deadline and giving a realistic alternative date. Send a copy to your opponent with a covering letter inviting them to agree to the new date.

FIXING THE DATE

The court will write to you with the hearing date. If you cannot make it on that date, you must write to the court as soon as possible (or at least a week before the hearing is due to take place), explaining the reason why you cannot attend. Make sure that you mark the top of your letter clearly with the hearing date and the case reference number. You should also enclose any evidence in support of your reason (for example, a letter from your GP if you are ill, or a

letter from your employer if you are going to be out of the country because of work). If there really is a good reason why you cannot get there, the court will fix a new date for the hearing.

Alternatively, you could tell the court to go ahead without you – but obviously that is a high-risk strategy and not one that is often adopted. However, the court will not postpone the hearing indefinitely and a second request is less likely to be granted.

"Keep communication with your opponent short and to the point, and make notes of any telephone conversations you have."

LEGAL REPRESENTATIVES

Although the small claims track is designed for claims where the parties have not got legal representation, there is nothing to stop someone from using a lawyer. It simply means they won't be able to claim back the cost of doing so if they win. It is not uncommon to get to court only to find the other side is represented by a solicitor or barrister. For example, insurance companies often use junior barristers to do road accident cases. If your contact with your opponent has been through solicitors, the chances are that they will use a legal representative for the hearing. Try not to be intimidated by this. The judge should make sure that the fact that you are not represented does not put you at a disadvantage.

WITNESS ARRANGEMENTS

You will need to arrange for anyone who has made a witness statement on your behalf to come to the hearing to give oral evidence. Arrange to meet them at least an hour before the hearing is due to start. If the court is in the town centre, you may prefer to meet up in a café nearby where you can have a coffee or tea and discuss the case in relative privacy. Make sure your witnesses read their statements before you go in to court.

You and your witnesses should aim to be at court at least half an hour before the start of the hearing.

MEETING YOUR OPPONENT

Unless your relationship with your opponent is very difficult, you should at least greet him or her on arrival and make sure that there is nothing more that can be agreed before you go in to see the judge. If you find the discussion is deteriorating into an argument, withdraw immediately, but if you can reach a last-minute agreement about how a particular loss is to be calculated or what facts are agreed, it will make everybody's life easier and will get the approval of the judge.

WAITING TO GET STARTED

In a large County Court your case will be announced over the tannoy system and an usher will direct you to the district judge's room. In a small court you may find it is more like going to see your doctor. You and your opponent sit in the waiting room until the judge calls you in over the intercom. Either way, the hearing will take place in the judge's office. You will find yourself sitting across the table from your opponent, with the judge at the head of the table. None of the formality you might associate with court hearings will apply. There is no standing up to give evidence, usually no one takes the oath and you are close enough to everyone for the hearing to be conducted at ordinary conversation level. The district judge will explain the procedure at the beginning and then guide you and your opponent through it, intervening if he or she considers it necessary to do so.

❝ If the hearing is in a small county court, it can feel more like going to see your doctor. ❞

 Preparing your case is just as important as presenting it – see pages 140-52. Information on final preparations is on pages 153-8.

PRESENTING YOUR CASE

If you have prepared your case in advance, you should be able to summarise the important points of evidence and arguments. You are bound to feel a little nervous when you first go in, but most judges go to great pains to ensure that litigants do not feel intimidated by the situation. If you do lose track of where you are or cannot find a document, just say so:

'I'm so sorry, I've lost my train of thought. I just need a minute to get back on track.'

Or

'The document I'm looking for is a letter dated 14 June, I'm just going to take a minute to find it.'

Try to make a note of anything your opponent says which either helps your case or damages theirs. You will not be able to write down everything he or she says – particularly when you are asking the questions – but anything that is different from what has been said before or any admission that he or she makes is worth noting and reminding the judge about when you make your closing comments.

In general terms, the claimant has to prove his or her case and so will usually go first with the defendant having the opportunity to give evidence in response and answer the allegations made by the claimant. Most hearings take between one and two hours. When the judge has heard each side's evidence and arguments, he or she will decide who has

Formalities

A male district judge is addressed as 'sir'. A female district judge is 'madam' or 'ma'am'.

won and give the reasons why. Sometimes the district judge will ask the parties to leave the room at the end of the hearing for about 20 minutes, in order to give him or her some space to give thought to the decision.

It is a good idea to try to take a written note of the district judge's decision. If you have a note of the judge's findings and reasons, it will help you understand why he or she came to the final decision. If you do want to consider an appeal, the notes may also help a solicitor to advise you whether or not you would have a good chance of succeeding.

" Most judges try very hard to ensure that litigants do not feel intimidated. If you've lost track of where you are in the case, say so. "

COSTS

Once the district judge has given the final decision, the only other thing to be discussed is costs. Normally this means that if the claimant has won, he or she will be awarded the costs of the court fee, witness expenses and, if appropriate, the cost of an expert's report. If the defendant has won, he or she will receive any witness and expert expenses.

Unreasonable conduct

If the winning party can persuade the judge that the loser has behaved unreasonably, then the judge may also decide to go beyond the usual costs limit of the small claims track and order the losing party to pay legal costs. Bringing or defending a claim unsuccessfully will not usually be regarded as unreasonable conduct. There really has to be something that goes

beyond the normal conduct of someone who has failed to prove or defend a civil claim. Having said that, there are no hard and fast rules and if you think your opponent has behaved unreasonably, there is nothing to stop you pointing this out to the judge and asking him or her to consider making a more generous costs order.

However, if you have done the case yourself, it may be that all your expenses will, in fact, be covered by the normal small claims track costs order. If you have incurred a lot of expense (for example, if your expert's report cost more than £200) and you think that you can show that your opponent has behaved unreasonably, it is a good idea to set out the extra costs in a schedule and provide copies to your opponent and the district judge at the hearing. The judge will decide there and then what costs the losing party should have to pay (this is

Examples of unreasonable conduct

- Fabricating a claim or a defence.

- Dishonesty.

- Failing to supply proper details of the claim or defence when ordered to do so by the court.

- Stating that a key document exists and then failing to produce it.

- Giving evidence at the hearing that directly contradicts your witness statement.

- Failing to take the court proceedings seriously.

- Failing to take any part in the proceedings.

Case Study | Lucrezia Duffell

Lucrezia Duffell claimed the cost of repairs to her car after a road accident. The other driver, Philip Davies, and his insurers failed to reply either to letters written on her behalf or the court proceedings. This was because Mr Davies had failed to co-operate with his insurance company. In the end, Ms Duffell entered judgment in default of a defence (see page 80) and there was a hearing to decide how much Mr Davies should pay. The district judge allowed £393.91 for the repairs to the car but refused to award her any costs other than those allowed on the small claims track, so she appealed. The appeal judge decided that the conduct of Mr Davies and his insurance company had been unreasonable and had left Ms Duffell with no choice but to bring a claim in the court. He allowed her appeal and ruled that she was entitled to legal costs because of the unreasonable conduct of the defendant.

Lucrezia Duffell v Philip Davies (18 February 2000) Liverpool County Court

known as a summary assessment of costs) and, if there has been an argument about how much the costs should be, will give brief reasons for the decision.

> **❝ If you have incurred a lot of expense and your opponent has been unreasonable, set out the extra costs and provide copies of them. ❞**

APPEALS

If you lose your case, you have a right of appeal. The first thing you should do is ask the district judge there and then for permission to appeal. You will be given the opportunity to explain why you want to appeal but it is very unlikely that the district judge will give you permission. To do so would suggest that the judge is uncertain whether the decision that he or she has just made was the right one, which is very rarely the case. Instead, you will have to ask for permission in writing from the court using form N161.

 See page 000 for the appeal procedure, which is the same for all three tracks.

SETTING ASIDE THE DECISION

If you were neither at the hearing nor represented, you can ask the court to set aside a judgment made against you and have another hearing as long as you apply within 14 days of receiving the letter from the court telling you about the judgment. However, the court will only agree to do this if:

- **You did not write to the court** in advance to say that you would not be there.
- **There is a good reason** as to why you didn't go or send someone else on your behalf.
- **You have 'a reasonable prospect of success'.** In other words, you must be able to show the court that this is not just a delaying tactic and that if you are given the chance to present your case, it may well turn out that judgment should not have been entered against you.

Although it will usually be the defendant who asks for a rehearing, the rule also applies to claimants who have missed the hearing for a reason they could not help.

Small claims track: a checklist

✓ Have all the directions made by the court been complied with?

✓ Have copies of the documents and witness statements you want to use at the hearing been sent both to the court and your opponent?

✓ Have you received documents and/or witness statements from your opponent and, if not, have you made a formal written request for them?

✓ Do you have the originals of the documents you want to use ready to take to court?

✓ Do you have two further copies of the documents you want to use just in case any of the ones you sent have gone astray?

✓ Have you told your witnesses when and where they should meet you on the day of the hearing?

✓ Do you (and your witnesses) have proof of travel expenses, loss of earnings and cost of overnight accommodation, which can be recovered if you win?

✓ Do you have the invoice for any expert report obtained?

Fast track claims

The fast track is designed for claims that are relatively straightforward. The court will work on the basis that a lot of the preparation necessary to get the case ready for trial has already been done before court proceedings were issued: particularly if the claim is covered by a pre-action protocol.

Both district judges and circuit judges can deal with fast track cases.

THE FAST TRACK IN A NUTSHELL

In a normal fast track case:

- **The value of the claim** is between £5,000 and £15,000 except in personal injury and housing disrepair cases where the claim will have a value of between £1,000 and £15,000.
- **The parties will have lawyers** acting for them.
- **The trial will not take more than a day.**
- **At the end of the trial**, the judge will decide there and then the amount of costs the losing side must pay the winner (this is known as a summary assessment of cost, see page 177).

GETTING A FAST TRACK CLAIM READY FOR TRIAL

Once a case has been allocated to the fast track, the court will make directions with the aim of having the case ready for trial within 30 weeks. In fact, the rules say that at the time the court gives these directions, it should either fix a date for the trial (although this is relatively unusual) or identify a three-week period during which the trial will take place.

This means that you ought to have your claim dealt with within eight months from the start of the proceedings. However, it is not unusual for the original trial period (or trial window) to be rescheduled to a later time if there is any delay in dealing with the directions the court has made.

❝ Fast track claims should be dealt with within eight months. ❞

 For the Civil Procedure Rules relating to fast track claims, see CPR Parts 28, 26.6(5) and 46.

Common directions in fast track and multi track claims

Direction	What happens
Standard disclosure of documents	Each side makes a list of all the documents that are or have been in their possession and which: - support their case - support the other side's case - adversely affect their case - adversely affect the other side's case
Exchange of witness statements of fact	Statements of all the witnesses whose evidence will be used at trial should be exchanged by the date specified
Jointly instructed expert report	Both sides are to share the cost of obtaining a report from an independent expert in the area of dispute
Or Each party has permission to obtain a report from an expert in a specified field or fields	Exchange of these reports may be delayed until after the exchange of witness statements so that each expert has a chance to comment on the other side's evidence

Jargon buster

Directions Orders made by the court that tell the parties what they have to do to get the case ready for trial

Multi track claims

Multi track claims come in all shapes and sizes. They range from relatively straightforward cases where the amount in dispute is just above the fast track limit, to complex commercial disputes where there are millions of pounds at stake. The procedures for dealing with multi track claims are designed to be flexible enough to deal with claims at either end of the spectrum.

MULTI TRACK CLAIMS IN A NUTSHELL

In a normal multi track case:

- **Particular importance** is attached to the overriding objective (see CPR Part 1)
- **The court plays a proactive part** in getting the case ready for trial. If things seem to be moving too slowly, the court can take the initiative to get things going by imposing strict deadlines or requiring the parties to come and explain what has been happening.
- **The parties are expected to co-operate** with each other as much as possible.
- **The court has a range of penalties** that can be imposed if either side does not comply with the directions. These include:
  - Paying money in to court.
  - Striking out all or part of a statement of case.
  - Barring a party from pursuing a particular argument if they fail to meet a new deadline.

- Where there has to be another hearing as a result of non-compliance, not allowing the party responsible to recover the costs of that hearing.
- **The parties have to give the court an estimate** of what their costs are likely to be, including the costs that they have incurred to date.
- **It is very likely that there will be at least one case management conference** during the course of the proceedings.
- **Circuit judges and High Court judges** usually deal with multi track trials.
- **District judges** deal with case management (preparations for trial) and can do a multi track trial as long as both sides agree to it.

❝ If a multi track case is taking too long, the court can take the initiative by imposing deadlines or requiring an explanation. ❞

GETTING A MULTI TRACK CLAIM READY FOR TRIAL

Like the other tracks, as soon as the case has been allocated to the multi track, a district judge considers what directions need to be made. In a case that is just above the fast track financial limit, the directions the court makes are likely to be virtually identical to those made for a fast track case. In more complicated cases, the court will arrange a case management conference (CMC), which the lawyers acting for the parties must attend; so that right at the outset the parties and the court can discuss the steps that need to be taken to get the claim ready for trial. If the case needs a lot of preparation, further CMCs will take place from time to time so that the court can monitor the claim's progress, ensure the parties are complying with the directions and deal with any problems that may arise.

When the case is nearly ready for trial, a further hearing known as a pre-trial review (PTR) will take place, again with the judge and the parties' lawyers, to ensure that everything will be in place for the date of the trial. If disagreements arise during preparing for the trial or the case is particularly complex, the barrister who is doing the trial will often be the one who deals with the CMC or PTR.

Unless you are dealing with the case yourself, you will not need to be there. Although if you are interested and have the time, there is nothing to stop you going along to see what happens.

> **ff As soon as the case has been allocated to the multi track, a district judge considers what directions need to be made. ??**

 For more information on case management conferences, see page 140.

Changing track

Although the value of the claim will normally decide which track a claim goes on to, either side can ask for it to go on a different track either on the allocation questionnaire or, if that doesn't work, by making an application to the court. In either case, the court will want to know the reason for requesting another track.

The usual reason for asking for a claim to be put on a different track is because it is more complicated than a run-of-the-mill small claim or fast track case. Moving from the small claims to the fast track means that the successful party will be able to get legal costs. Moving from the fast track to the multi track means that higher costs can be claimed by the winning side and a more generous approach is taken by the court to expensive items such as expert evidence. It's not unusual for both sides to agree that the claim needs to move up a track, although the court will always have the last word and even where the parties agree, the district judge will still need to be persuaded to depart from the normal rule.

If one or both sides want to change track, the CPR say that the following matters should be taken into account:

- Financial value of the claim (not including legal costs or interest).

- What remedy is being asked for.
- How complex the claim is in terms of facts, evidence and the law.
- The number of parties involved.
- The value of any counterclaim or Part 20 claim (see page 69).
- How much evidence from witnesses at trial there is likely to be.

 If the parties to a claim want to take advantage of the more informal procedure and limits on costs liability available on the small claims track, there is nothing to stop them agreeing that that is where it should be dealt with. They will need the consent of the court to do this, but this is usually readily forthcoming.

 For the Civil Procedure Rules relating to changing court, see CPR Part 30.

- **Whether the claim has a wider importance** for people not directly involved in the proceedings.
- **What the parties' views are** (note that this comes a long way down the list).
- **The circumstances of the parties** (such as their financial circumstances).

COST IMPLICATIONS

Where a claim changes track, costs are awarded as follows:

- **From the start of proceedings to the date of transfer**: the costs applicable to the track it was originally allocated to.
- **From the date of transfer to the end of the case**: the cost rules for the new track will apply.

For example, the winner of a claim that started on the small claims track and was reallocated to the fast track after the exchange of witness statements, will not be entitled to legal costs for the stages up to and including the exchange of the statements.

RESISTING A CHANGE

If you are doing the claim yourself, you will have good reason for wanting the claim to stay on the small claims track, where even if you lose, you won't be paying your opponent's legal costs. It is not unknown for large corporations to try to get a claim moved on to the fast track in the hope that the risk of having to pay costs will deter the claimant from going any further with the claim. If you are facing this sort of David and Goliath situation, you should be able to rely upon the court to see through this ploy. If the claim is moved off the small claims track in the face of your opposition, you can be reasonably certain that there are good reasons for deciding that legal representation is necessary and if you haven't previously taken any legal advice, now is the time to do so.

CHANGING COURT

The claimant can choose to issue the claim either in the County Court or the High Court. However, the defendant may have a different opinion as to which court the case should be in, and if the claimant won't agree to a transfer, can make an application to have it moved. The main reason for moving from High Court to County Court is that the claim does not need the expertise of the High Court and County Court proceedings are usually cheaper. On the other hand, it may be necessary to move a particularly complicated case from the County Court to the High Court.

The application can be made at any point before the trial date is fixed and is made to the court currently dealing with the case. It is also possible that even if the parties are agreed where the case should be heard, the court will have a different view and may either turn down a joint request for a transfer, or transfer the claim to the court where the district judge dealing with the file thinks it should be heard. If you feel strongly that the court has got it wrong, you can ask for a hearing to argue why it should either stay where it is or move to another court.

The same rules apply for transferring a claim to the same type of court but in a different place.

Settlement

The vast majority of claims started in the civil courts are settled before they get to trial. The main, and very good reason for this, is that in most cases there will be an element of risk on both sides. Even if mediation or other attempts at alternative dispute resolution have not been successful, there is nothing to stop the parties from trying to negotiate a settlement even while they are continuing to prepare for trial.

ASSESSING THE RISK

Whether you have a solicitor acting for you or you are dealing with the claim yourself, you will need to give careful thought to how far you are willing to go to reach an agreement with your opponent. To do this you may find it helpful to take a long, hard look at how risky it would be to go to trial. Start by making a list of all the strengths and weak points of your case. First look at the evidence:

- Is there any documentary evidence that either supports your account of what happened or seems to contradict it?
- Are there any independent witnesses (including experts) who either support or contradict your case?
- If you are relying on friends or family to give evidence on your behalf, how well are they likely to cope with the pressure of giving evidence at a formal public hearing and, possibly, having to deal with hostile questioning?
- How clearly do you remember what happened?

❝ Take a long, hard look at how risky it will be to take the case to trial. Is it worth it? ❞

Next, you need to think about the value of the claim:

- **If you are the claimant,** do you have receipts or other proof of any expenses or losses you are claiming?
- **If you are the defendant,** is it likely that you will be able to show that the claimant is exaggerating any of his or her financial losses?
- **What advice has your solicitor** given you about what you can realistically expect to get or have to pay on a best-case and worst-case scenario?

If there is a claim for some other remedy as well as or instead of damages, is it likely that the court will grant it? For example, if you are suing your neighbour because he built an extension to his house a metre over your side of the boundary, unless the effect of it being there means that access to your back garden is completely obstructed, it is very unlikely that the court will order him to demolish it, even if you win. On the other hand, if the same neighbour has been making your life a misery by playing loud music in the early hours of the morning, the court will be more than willing to make an order forbidding him from continuing to disturb you.

Your solicitor will be able to advise you about all the possible outcomes. Lawyers are used to assessing the chance of success using a rough-and-ready percentage figure. If your claim is funded by a CFA or legal aid, your solicitor, and possibly barrister, will already have done a risk assessment and decided how vulnerable you are. They will also be able to advise you whether there are any legal issues that make the claim more risky to pursue or defend.

When lawyers assess the risk factor in a civil claim they always allow something for the **risks of litigation**. In other words, the possibility, even in the most rock-solid case, that something will go unexpectedly and horribly wrong. There really is no such thing as a cast-iron case until the moment the judge pronounces final judgment in your favour.

FINDING A COMPROMISE

Once you have ascertained how confident you feel, you can start to work out your parameters for settlement and this is something you will want to discuss with your solicitor. Obviously the greater the risk, the more you will need to be willing to compromise in any negotiations. It also helps to try to see the claim from your opponent's point of view. If it really looks as if the case might go either way, you will both have

Jargon buster

Without prejudice Making a concession or offer of settlement, which the trial judge will not know about if the claim goes to trial

every incentive to try and sort something out. If you're feeling pretty confident, try to look for ways of making a small concession that may allow your opponent to save face. There are very few situations (especially once proceedings have been started) where refusing to compromise at all will lead to complete capitulation by the other side.

“ Decide your parameters for settlement and discuss them with your solicitor. Study the claim from your opponent's viewpoint. ”

 <del>For more information on risk assessment and CFAs, see page 42.</del>
For more information on risk assessment and CFAs, see page 42.

TACTICS

There's no magic formula for negotiating a settlement. Unless there is a genuine willingness to compromise on both sides, any talks will be doomed to failure. This means putting on one side any anger that you may feel for your opponent – however justified – and exploring whether there is any common ground between you (even if this is limited to each side wanting to save face and/or further legal costs). If you are doing the negotiations yourself:

- **Encourage your opponent** to get the ball rolling by making the first offer (you can indicate an interest in settling the claim without giving anything away: 'I would be willing to consider any sensible offer you put forward'). This will enable you to find out how far apart you are without showing your hand.
- **While you might want to remind your opponent** of the strengths in your case ('My case is supported by the evidence of Mrs Rogers who is entirely independent'), do not allow the negotiation to deteriorate into a series of accusation and counter accusation, which will only heighten the bad feeling between you and make compromise increasingly hard to reach.
- **Keep something in reserve.** Do not put in your best and final offer first time round. On the other hand, do not drip-feed the negotiation with endless minuscule variations in your offer. Your opponent will quickly come to the conclusion that you're not really serious about reaching a settlement.
- **Do not say,** 'This is absolutely my last and final offer' unless you mean it. If you make a series of 'last and final offers', your opponent will not take the threat – or your negotiating skills – seriously. On the other hand, if you do make it clear that an offer does represent your bottom line and this produces an offer from your opponent that, although less than you wanted, is acceptable, don't have any qualms about taking it.

If you do reach agreement, it is very important to make sure that the terms of the agreement are absolutely clear. If the settlement involves payment of money, this should not be a problem, but if it means that the defendant has to take certain steps (for example, to put right defective building works), it is important to specify exactly what has to be done and the timescale for doing it.

❝ Make the first offer but keep something in reserve, while reminding your opponent of the strength of your case. ❞

'DROP HANDS' AGREEMENTS

Things can change dramatically during the course of the proceedings. A case that started off looking very good may suddenly get into trouble once the witness statements have been exchanged or a damaging document comes to light. If that happens to your case, you or your lawyer will have to try to get out of the proceedings on the best terms possible.

If it is your claim, this may mean agreeing with your opponent not to take the claim any further with each side paying their own legal costs. This is known as a 'drop hands' or 'walk away' agreement. The advantage is that you don't have to pay your opponent's legal costs, which is what would happen if you simply told the court that you wanted to withdraw or discontinue your claim, or continued to trial and lost. If there are real doubts as to whether you can win and the defendant offers a 'drop hands' agreement, you will need to give it careful consideration and if you have a CFA or legal expenses insurance, you may find that the insurer will insist on you accepting the offer.

ADVICE THAT'S HARD TO SWALLOW

It can be very difficult if you find yourself in a situation where you are being given very clear advice by your lawyers that you should accept an offer, which you really don't want to. If there is enough time and it has not already been done, you should ask your solicitor – or barrister – to set out in writing why he or she thinks you should accept the offer. If you remain unconvinced by the arguments, ask for a face-to-face meeting where you can discuss the options. It can help to take a partner or friend along who will be able to discuss what's been said with you afterwards.

Do not make any final decision at the meeting itself, but say that you need a little time to think things over. However, if there is pressure of time, you will need to reach a decision and tell your solicitor what it is as soon as possible. You may find that you are left with the choice of accepting the offer or going it alone if the effect of saying no is that the funding for your claim will be withdrawn. You can opt to get a second opinion (see page 137) but if that supports the original advice you have been given, you really will need to be very sure of your position to carry on alone.

For more information about legal expenses insurance (or 'before the event' insurance), see page 48.

Settlement

PART 36 OFFERS

A Part 36 offer is a formal offer of settlement that either party can make. If you do turn down a Part 36 offer and the claim goes to trial, unless you end up in a better position than if you had accepted the offer, there will be a costs penalty. The idea is that if the offer had been accepted, all the expense of going to trial would have been saved. The court shows its disapproval of this waste of time and money by making the party who rejected the offer pay all the costs

How a Part 36 offer works

- The claimant or the defendant makes a formal written offer giving the other side 21 days from the date the offer is received to decide whether to accept or not.
- If the offer is accepted, the court is informed and the proceedings are stayed indefinitely. The person accepting the offer is also entitled to their legal costs up to the date the offer was accepted on a standard basis unless costs are expressly excluded from the offer.
- If the offer is refused and the party to whom it was made does not beat the offer at trial, they must pay as follows.

The defendant who has failed to beat the claimant's offer must pay:

- Extra interest on the damages awarded by the court, of up to 10 per cent above base rate from the last day the offer could have been accepted. The judge will decide the rate and for how long the extra interest should be paid.
- Costs on an indemnity basis from the last day the offer could have been accepted.
- Interest on those extra costs of up to 10 per cent above base rate, again decided by the judge.

The claimant who has failed to beat the defendant's offer must pay:

- The defendant's legal costs from the last day on which the offer could be accepted.
- Interest on those costs (although the rate is not specified).
- Their own legal costs, including the costs of trial, from the last date the money could have been accepted.

 For the Civil Procedure Rules relating to Part 36 offers, see CPR Parts 36 and 44(3)(4).

incurred after the deadline for accepting the offer passed.

If you are defending a claim, making a formal Part 36 offer is one of the most effective ways of putting pressure on the claimant to settle on your terms. CPR Part 36 makes detailed rules for both claimants and defendants to make formal offers of settlement; but the claimant is always more at risk under a Part 36 offer. The cost of getting it wrong might be enough to swallow all or most of any damages awarded by the court; and, in a difficult case, it may be a matter of choosing between taking a settlement that is much lower than you would get if you were to win or taking the risk of getting nothing at all.

If you are on the receiving end of a Part 36 offer and you turn it down, only to do less well at trial, you will not only have to live with the uncomfortable fact that you would have been better off accepting your opponent's offer and avoiding the stress of a court hearing, but you will also be penalised financially by the court. Since deciding whether or not to accept a Part 36 offer depends upon being able to second-guess what will happen if the claim goes to trial, at times it may feel as if you are on a TV game show, trying to guess how much money is in the box. The only way to minimise the risk is to try to take a long, hard look at the strengths and weakness of your case and listen to the advice your solicitor or barrister gives you. Ultimately, whether or not ` you are legally represented, it must be your decision.

Part 36 offers in personal injury cases

If the claim is for personal injury in a case where the claimant has been receiving state benefits as a result of the injury, or provisional damages or a structured settlement is on offer, special rules about how the offer should be formulated apply and you really will need a lawyer to deal with it for you.

If a claimant who has turned down a Part 36 offer in a high value claim is awarded damages that are only just above the defendant's Part 36 offer, the court may still decide to reduce the amount of costs the claimant is entitled to. This will probably be the most likely outcome if the costs of taking the claim to trial far outweigh the extra money that the claimant has recovered at trial.

Small claims track

Part 36 offers cannot be made in cases that have been allocated to the small claims track, although there are no other restrictions on trying to settle a small claim.

Ask the expert

I am claiming damages of £65,000 from the bank's surveyor who failed to notice structural defects when he carried out a mortgage valuation of our house. We have had a Part 36 offer of £50,000, which my solicitor is advising me to accept. I understand that if I take the money, the court proceedings will be stayed. Does this mean that if further problems come to light I can go back to court and use these proceedings to claim further damages from him?

No. If you accept the current offer it will settle once and for all your claim arising out of the survey that he carried out on your property. Although theoretically court proceedings are only stayed, or put on hold, in practical terms the action will come to an end. The only reason you could revive the proceedings would be if the surveyor failed to pay the money. In fact, that should not be a problem because he will almost certainly have insurance to cover any claim against him made for professional negligence. If, however, he does not pay, you can ask the court to enforce the settlement agreement. Your claim against him will be for the £50,000 that you agreed to accept. You will not be able to claim the £65,000 you were originally asking for.

How to make a Part 36 offer

The rules say that if you want to make a formal Part 36 offer it must be in writing and must say:

- That the offer is made under CPR Part 36.
- That you intend the offer to have the consequences set out in CPR Part 36.
- Whether the offer relates to all of the claim or just part of it (if it is just part of the claim, you must make it clear which part you intend your offer to apply to).
- Whether the offer takes into account any counterclaim or Part 20 claim (see page 69).
- Whether the offer takes into account any interim payment.
- That the person you are making the offer to has at least 21 days to decide whether to accept it (you can allow more time if you want, but you must make it clear when the deadline is).

If you are making an offer that includes acceptance or payment of a sum of money, unless you state otherwise, it will be assumed that your offer includes interest.

The most important thing is to make sure that the terms of the offer are absolutely clear. If you are doing it yourself, ask someone else to read the letter before you send it and tell you what they think the offer consists of.

Claimant's Part 36 offers

It is less common for a claimant to make a Part 36 offer, mainly because the financial penalty for failing to beat a claimant's offer is not so severe as the other way round. Nevertheless, it can be very sensible for a claimant to spell out at a relatively early stage what they would be prepared to accept in settlement of the claim.

Defendant's Part 36 offers

Before 6 April 2007, if a defendant wanted to make an offer to settle a claim for damages, he or she had to show that they were good for the money by paying the full amount excluding costs in to court. The court would then hold the money until either the claimant accepted it or the end of the proceedings. This is no longer necessary. The defendant only has to put the offer in writing. However, if the claimant accepts it, the full amount (but not costs) must be paid within 14 days. If the money is not forthcoming, the claimant can ask the court to enter judgment against the defendant for the amount agreed and then try to get the money through enforcement proceedings (see pages 192–7).

> " A Part 36 offer can't be withdrawn or changed without court permission during the 21-day acceptance period. "

Payment date

If you receive an offer that is less than you might get at trial and you have doubts about the defendant's ability to pay, you can make it a condition of acceptance that the full amount is paid within 14 days. If the money is not forthcoming, you will then be free to continue with your claim for the full amount.

Changing your mind

Changing you mind about a Part 36 offer has implications it is as well to be aware of.

- **About making an offer** Once a Part 36 offer has been made, during the 21 days allowed for acceptance, the party making it cannot withdraw the offer or change it to one that is not so good, unless the court gives its permission. The court is unlikely to do this unless something has happened that dramatically affects the likely outcome of the case; for example, if evidence comes to light during the 21-day period that suggests the claimant has exaggerated the value of the claim. Once the deadline for accepting the offer has passed you are free to withdraw or vary your offer however you want to.
- **About accepting the offer** If, on the other hand, you have refused a Part 36 offer and decide after the time for accepting it has passed that you want

to accept it after all, unless your opponent agrees, you will also need to ask the permission of the court. The court may refuse to let you do so, if, in the meantime, something has happened that adversely affects your chance of winning the case. If you do want to accept an offer after the deadline, the usual rule is that you will have to pay your opponent's costs from the last day you could have accepted it. This means that if you are having second thoughts about accepting an offer that you previously turned down, the sooner you do something about it the better. The more time that passes, the greater the amount of costs that you will have to pay.

Part 36 offers made less than 21 days before the trial

If you fail to beat a Part 36 offer made less than 21 days before the trial, it will really be up to the judge to decide, taking into account the circumstances of your particular case, whether there should be any costs penalty. If the reality of the situation is that it was a good offer and you had ample time to consider it (more than a week or so), you may well be at risk of having to pay the costs of the trial.

Ask the expert

I am making a claim against my builder for the shoddy job he made of building our extension. He has made a Part 36 offer to settle the case by paying £10,000. As we effectively had to have the whole thing rebuilt at a cost of over £25,000 this seems far too low. Our solicitor tells us we have a good case, which we ought to win if we go to trial, and certainly the joint expert has come down in our favour. However, I really do want this sorted out as soon as possible and I find the thought of having to go to court in a few months time really stressful. Now that he's made a formal Part 36 offer, does that stop us from making one back?

No. Both sides can make as many Part 36 offers as they want to during the course of the proceedings. It sounds as if you can turn down the current offer with reasonable confidence. You may find that once you have rejected it, your opponent will make an improved Part 36. Alternatively, you can take the initiative and make your own Part 36 offer. As you have a good case, you could offer to settle your claim for £22,500, offering your builder, in effect, a 10 per cent discount and the chance to avoid having to pay all the legal costs of a multi track trial. If that offer is rejected, you could always make another Part 36 offer of settlement at £20,000. However, if that is not accepted and you really do have a good case, you probably should not go any lower.

Case Study   James Jackson

James Jackson, the claimant, was a 17-year-old recruit in the Royal Engineers when he badly injured his right knee during a training exercise. He sued the Ministry of Defence (MoD), the defendant, claiming £1 million in compensation. The MoD accepted liability but disputed the amount claimed. Two months before the trial to assess damages took place, the defendant made a Part 36 offer of £150,000, which the claimant rejected. There was also a meeting between the parties a month before the trial to try to settle the case, but no agreement was reached.

At trial, the claimant abandoned many of the claims for financial loss that he had originally made. Even so, the judge decided that he had exaggerated the effect of the injury and awarded him only £155,000 in damages. The defendant tried to argue that the court should take into account the negotiations that took place during the settlement meeting. The MoD said that if the claimant had been willing then to settle the claim for £155,000, there would have been no need for a trial. Both the trial judge and the Court of Appeal completely rejected the idea that anything said during a settlement meeting could have any effect on what order for costs was made at trial. The Court of Appeal said that if the defendant had wanted to, it could have made a small increase in its Part 36 offer. However, the court did reduce the claimant's costs by 25 per cent because, despite starting off with such a big claim, he had only just beaten the Part 36 offer.

James Jackson v Ministry of Defence (2006) EWCA Civ 46

Obtaining permission

You will need permission from the court if:

- You want to change or withdraw a Part 36 offer before the deadline for accepting it has expired.
- You want to accept a Part 36 offer after the deadline for accepting it has passed and the party who made the offer does not agree.
- You want to accept a Part 36 offer after the trial has actually started.
- The claim is for or against a child or someone who is not able to make decisions because of a learning disability or medical condition.

TOMLIN ORDERS

If the defendant loses the case, a High Court or County Court judgment will be entered against him or her, which is likely to have an immediate and devastating effect on credit rating. A Part 36 offer – if it is accepted – is one way of avoiding this. As long as the defendant pays the money, the action effectively comes to an end without judgment being entered. Another way of achieving the same result, if an agreement has been reached without using Part 36, is to draw up a Tomlin order (named after the judge who first came up with the idea).

The parties set out all the terms of their agreement in a separate schedule, which is attached to the court order. The order itself simply states:

- The court proceedings are stayed to allow the terms agreed in the schedule to be put into effect.
- The costs order that the parties have agreed upon.

Case Study   Frank West

Frank West died intestate in 1989 and a family dispute erupted over his estate involving his second wife and the children of his first and second marriages. Eventually the case went to court. In 1996, a settlement was reached and a Tomlin order was drawn up. Under the schedule it was agreed that Jeffrey, who was the son of the first marriage, should be paid various sums of money in respect of his claim against his father's estate. Rosemary, who was also a child of the first marriage, was the third defendant to the claim. She had been present in court, though not legally represented, when the Tomlin order was made and had signed the order.

In fact, there was not enough money in the estate to pay Jeffrey and not surprisingly the agreement broke down.

The case came back to court over six years later. Rosemary argued that she was not bound by the agreement because she had been misled into signing the order on the basis that it was a form to show that she had been present in court.

The judge found that since she had never applied to the court to set aside the order nor was she willing to make a formal application even then, she was bound by the Tomlin order. He thought it unlikely that she really did not know what she was signing and said she should either put up or shut up and that, in any case, it was probably too late for her to ask the court to set aside the order as it was over six years since it was made, so the limitation deadline had passed.

West v West & 2 Others (2002) EWHC 2778 (CH)

The court does not need to approve – or even look at – the terms in the schedule. The schedule is treated as a binding legal agreement between the parties, which effectively brings the court proceedings to an end. If the agreement is not honoured, then the agreement can be enforced through the court and is treated in the same way as any other claim for breach of contract.

Sticking points – Costs

Sometimes it is possible to agree most of the matters in dispute, leaving just one or two issues unresolved. The most common sticking point is costs. It is not unusual for the parties to agree a compromise in principle but to each hold out on costs. If the negotiations are taking place at the door of the court, the simplest solution is to ask the judge who was going to hear the case to decide what costs order should be made. Otherwise, it will be a matter of arranging a hearing just to deal with the matters that cannot be agreed upon. If the only point in dispute is costs, this may be a high-risk strategy since the costs of the hearing may in themselves outweigh the amount at stake.

SETTING ASIDE A SETTLEMENT

Once an agreement has been reached and recorded in writing, either through correspondence or a Tomlin order, everyone who is a party to it will be bound by its terms. You will only be able to get out of it if you can show:

Misrepresentation That you were misled by your opponent into agreeing to something which, if you had known the real situation, you would never have agreed to.

Mistake – either that both parties were at cross-purposes or that one side, through no fault of their own, was completely mistaken about what was being agreed to. A mistake about a detail of the agreement will not be enough. It must be something that has the effect of making the settlement completely different to the one you thought were agreeing to.

Duress That you only signed the agreement because you were under so much pressure or were subjected to threats from your opponent. The pressure must be so great that it effectively meant you were unable to make an informed decision about whether or not to accept the terms of the agreement.

For more information on the subject of awarding costs, see pages 175-80, which explains how they are awarded and calculated.

Settlement

If, at the time you signed the agreement, you had legal representation, it will be almost impossible to make a case for having the agreement set aside unless your lawyers were also misled.

SETTLING AN APPEAL

Although it is less common, there is nothing to stop the parties to an appeal from trying to reach a settlement, including making a Part 36 offer, which will have the same effect, if it is not beaten, as one made before the trial. If you have won your case at trial, you may be reluctant to make any concession to your opponent and the odds are stacked firmly in your favour (see Chapter 9). However, if your opponent has succeeded in getting permission from the court to appeal the decision, and your solicitor is concerned that the judge may have got it wrong – which does sometimes happen – you may need to give serious consideration to reopening negotiations with the other side. Appeals can be very expensive and if the decision is completely reversed, you will then find yourself paying for the entire costs of the proceedings.

&& If your opponent gets permission to appeal and your solicitor thinks the judge may have got it wrong, you may need to re-open negotiations. "

Evidence

From an early stage you or your solicitor will need to assemble evidence to support your case if the claim goes to trial. This will be in the form of documents, witness statements of fact and expert reports. When the court makes directions setting out the timetable for preparing the claim for trial, it will set a date by which each type of evidence must be ready to send to your opponent.

Documents

Documents form an important part of the evidence because they can often show what was going on before there was any thought of court proceedings. They can corroborate or contradict witness evidence and are often used extensively in cross-examination.

The following are examples of the kind of documents that are likely to feature in civil claims:

- Estimates, quotations or written agreements exchanged between the parties.
- Correspondence between the parties before the dispute arose.
- Correspondence between the parties after the dispute arose.
- Letters and/or documents from other people that are relevant to the dispute.
- Minutes of meetings.
- Property or trust deeds.
- Tenancy agreements.
- Medical records.

- Police reports of any criminal investigation and/or certificate of conviction.
- Accident investigation or Health and Safety Executive reports.
- Documents confirming expenses or financial loss, such as repair estimates, wage slips and tax returns.

Jargon buster

Disclosure Process of giving the other party access to any documents that are relevant to the claim

Inspection Making the documents on the list that are not privileged available to the other party

Lists Listing all the documents in the possession or control of a party (whether or not they are privileged)

Non-party disclosure Disclosure of documents held by someone who is not a party to the claim

Pre-action disclosure Disclosure before proceedings have started

Privilege Protection from disclosure

Waive Give up/relinquish

❝Standard disclosure is the first thing the parties have to do in most fast and multi track claims.❞

STANDARD DISCLOSURE

In most fast track and multi track claims, the first thing the parties will have to do under the directions is to provide what is known as standard disclosure. This involves making a list of all the documents that were or are in your possession or control (documents that you are entitled to have access to or make copies of) and which:

Unless specific allegations of fraud have been made against you, you do not have to disclose documents that may incriminate you.

- Support your case.
- Are damaging to your opponent's case.
- Are damaging to your case.
- Support your opponent's case.

The parties must then exchange their lists by the deadline set by the court.

Small claims track

If your claim has been allocated to the small claims track you won't need to worry about preparing a formal disclosure list. The only documents you need to send to your opponent and the court are those that you want to rely on, but don't forget that you will need to take the originals to court for the final hearing. Although you can't make an application for specific disclosure, if you think your opponent has a document that might have a bearing on the case, there is nothing to stop you from writing and asking him or her for it. If it's still not forthcoming, you can raise the matter at the final hearing.

Once you have each other's lists, you can then ask for copies of any of the documents you want to see, except those that are privileged. You will have to pay photocopying costs.

Equally, you will have to provide copies of any documents on your list that your opponent asks for, except, again, for those that are privileged.

Privileged documents

Some documents may be relevant to the dispute but are considered to be private or privileged. They must be included on the disclosure list but the other side is not entitled to see them or ask for copies. The most common documents that fall within the definition of privilege are any documents relating to the legal proceedings, including correspondence with your solicitor about the claim, written advice from your solicitor or a barrister and other reports or investigations that were carried out once it became apparent that there were likely to be court proceedings. If the parties disagree about whether or not a document is privileged, an application to the court will have to be made and the district judge will decide.

121

Just because a document is confidential or contains personal or sensitive information about someone or something not directly involved in the dispute, does not make it privileged. If there is information about other people that would normally be confidential, it may be possible to provide copies pf the documents with the names blacked out.

Specific disclosure

If there are reasons for thinking that your opponent has documents that are relevant to the claim and which have not been included in the standard disclosure list, you can apply to the court for specific disclosure. You will need to support your application with a statement explaining what documents you want and why their disclosure is necessary for there to be a fair disposal of the claim.

Case Study | David and Victoria Beckham

David and Victoria Beckham sued the *News of the World* for libel when it published an article alleging that they presented a false public image and that really their marriage was in trouble. The newspaper applied for specific disclosure of a number of documents including those relating to a commercial arrangement they had with a member of the paparazzi, a family skiing holiday in France, mobile phone records, information concerning David Beckham's move to Madrid, and the unedited version of 'The Real Beckhams', a fly-on-the-wall documentary.

The Beckhams agreed to try and obtain some itemised mobile phone bills. The judge also directed that they should 'use their best endeavours' to find out from the film makers if the documentary footage contained any incidents, such as rows between the couple, that the newspaper alleged had taken place during filming. Otherwise, all the other requests by the newspaper for specific disclosure were refused, because they were not necessary for a fair trial to take place.

The Beckhams also applied for specific disclosure. They wanted the notes and tape recordings made by journalists who had interviewed their former nanny. The judge ordered the newspaper to disclose them. He said they were relevant because the court would need to look at everything she had told the journalists in order to decide whether it was in the public interest, as the newspaper alleged, for the story to be published. The disclosure might also help the court to decide whether the nanny could be believed.

Beckham v News Group Newspapers Limited (2005) EWHC 2252 QB

Waiving privilege

If part of a document that would otherwise be privileged is shown to the court or the other side, privilege is regarded as having been given up – or waived – and your opponent becomes entitled to see the whole document. However, if it is obvious that a privileged document has been given to you by mistake, you are expected to return it and will not be allowed to use any information it contained.

"If part of a privileged document is shown, its privileged status is regarded as being waived, unless it was shown or given by mistake."

Disclosure statements

If you are preparing the list yourself, your list should end with the following statements:

'I, the above named claimant/defendant, state that I have carried out a reasonable and proportionate search to locate all the documents that I am required to disclose under the order made by the court on ... (insert date of directions order).

'I did not search for ... (state any categories of document you have not searched or ways in which you limited the search, for example,

- Documents before ...
- Documents located elsewhere other than ...)

'I certify that I understand the duty of disclosure and to the best of my knowledge I have carried out that duty. I certify that the above list is a complete list of all the documents which are or have been in my control and which I am obliged under the said order to disclose.'

To read the full written judgment for the case study opposite, go to www.bailii.org.uk where all High Court decisions are listed by the year and in alphabetical order (see also page 19 for more information about using the internet for judgments).

Ask the expert

I injured my back badly in an accident at work and I'm making a personal injury claim against my employer. They are fighting the case all the way. They say that the accident didn't happen in the way I described and that I'm exaggerating how bad the injury is. I have an independent medical report from a doctor who has seen all my medical records, which supports me. Now my solicitor has asked me to sign for the release of my medical records to their solicitor. I really don't want to do this.

There's a lot of very personal information, which has nothing to do with my back. I've suffered from depression on and off since my twenties and I've also had marital problems. I never let these things interfere with my work so my employer knows nothing about any of this. Do I have to give them access to this confidential information or can we at least blank out the bits that don't relate to my back? And what use can they make of them if I do disclose the records?

Unfortunately, if you want to continue with your claim, you probably will have to disclose your medical records without editing them in any way. You cannot be forced to release them, but if you refuse, your employer's solicitor can make an application to the court for the proceedings to be halted until the records are disclosed. If the defendants intend to get their own medical report, their doctor is entitled to have the same information as yours.

Even if the defendants aren't getting their own medical report, they are still entitled to see the records so that they can put questions to your doctor. Their solicitor will want to explore the possibility that your previous medical history has some bearing on your current state of health and your capacity for work, both now and in the future, as this may have a significant effect on the value of your claim.

They may also want to compare the details given about the accident and symptoms in your medical records with your account of what happened. Any discrepancies can be used to suggest that your evidence is not reliable; although this may simply be the result of inaccurate note-taking by the doctor concerned.

Any reluctance on your part to disclose the records will be treated as evidence that you have something to hide. It's better to agree and then spend time going through the notes to double-check that they record accurately the information you gave to your doctors. If there are any mistakes, your solicitor will need to highlight them as soon as possible. The only slight saving grace is that your employer cannot use the information contained in the records for any purpose other than testing your personal injury claim.

Witness statements of fact

Although it does happen, there are very few claims in which everyone is agreed about the facts. This means that in most cases the judge at trial will have to decide which version of events he or she thinks is more likely.

That decision will be based on:

- Looking at the documents.
- Reading the written witness statements.
- Listening to the witnesses at trial give their evidence and be cross-examined.

It goes without saying that the more the various types of your evidence support one another, the more likely the judge is to find in your favour. On the other hand, minor discrepancies in the evidence will not necessarily be fatal to your claim. Indeed, the judge may become suspicious if everything seems too pat and perfect. Life is an untidy business and occasional contradictions or gaps in the evidence will not worry a judge too much as long as you and your witnesses give an account that is broadly consistent with the documents and each other's evidence.

Any witness who is going to give oral evidence at trial, including the claimant and the defendant, will need to make and sign a statement setting out the evidence that he or she is going to give at court.

It is important that the evidence in the witness statements is relevant to the specific circumstances surrounding your claim. The court will not be interested in hearing about other disputes involving your opponent. The evidence of witnesses who are completely independent is particularly useful.

If someone can give evidence that is helpful to your case but is unable or unwilling to give evidence at trial, you can still submit a witness statement from him or her, but the evidence contained in it will be of limited value (see Hearsay Evidence, on page 126).

❝ Minor discrepancies needn't be fatal: indeed, evidence that seems too perfect arouses suspicion. ❞

CHANGING YOUR STORY

Your solicitor will have obtained a detailed account of what happened from you at the first meeting and used that, along with any documents available and information from other witnesses, to draft the formal letter before action or – if you are defending – your response to the claim. By the time the deadline for the exchange of witness statements approaches, the information that you originally provided will have been supplemented by your opponent's documents and any further investigations your solicitor has carried out.

You can expect your solicitor to press hard for an explanation about any inconsistencies that have come to light. He or she would not be doing their job properly if all the evidence wasn't examined critically. If there are things you have forgotten or got wrong the first time round, your witness statement gives you a chance to put the record straight and provide an explanation that should limit the potential for hostile questioning at trial. However, if there are major discrepancies between the other documents and your version of events, this may put you at real risk of losing the case. If this does happen, your solicitor will advise you how serious the risk is and what, if anything, can be done to put things right.

HEARSAY EVIDENCE

Hearsay evidence is second-hand evidence. If someone tells you about something that they have seen or heard, but you did not witness it yourself, it will be treated as hearsay and therefore of less value than evidence of which you have direct first-hand knowledge.

If you want to rely on a written statement from someone who is not able to give oral evidence at the trial, that will also be treated as hearsay evidence. Strictly speaking, a notice of hearsay evidence should be served on your opponent, although the judge will usually be willing to consider it even if this has not been done.

References to what other people have told you can also be included in your witness statement as long as they are relevant to specific circumstances of the claim.

The court will almost always allow you to refer to hearsay evidence in a civil trial, but the judge will be careful to draw a clear distinction between hearsay evidence (which cannot be tested by cross-examination) and direct evidence of what the witnesses have seen or heard for themselves.

Usually, unless the hearsay evidence is corroborated by documents or other evidence from witnesses, it will not carry much weight or make much difference to the judge's decision.

❝ If you forgot things or got something wrong the first time round, your witness statement offers a chance to put the record straight. ❞

The glossary on pages 204-9 explains the legal words and phrases that you will come across in the course of making a civil claim.

DECIDING WHAT'S RELEVANT

Whether you're doing the witness statements yourself or giving your solicitor the raw material to do the job for you, the real art of preparing a witness statement is deciding what should go in and what is better left out. A long rambling statement will soon lose the attention of the judge and anyone else reading it. On the other hand, a statement that skips over important but inconvenient facts will seem evasive.

THE FORMALITIES

The rules and practice directions say that in fast track and multi track claims, the witness statements must be set out in a certain way. In particular they must:

- Be on A4 paper with a 3.5cm margin, using one side of the sheet only.
- Preferably be typed but, in any event, be legible.
- Have numbered pages.
- Be divided into numbered paragraphs.
- Express all numbers and dates in figures.
- Set out the full name, address and occupation of the witness.
- If the witness is the claimant or the defendant or an employee of either party, say so.
- Identify and number consecutively any documents or photographs exhibited to the statement (for example, 'I refer to the letter of 12 May 2007 marked **DAB.1** and to the invoice it contained marked **DAB.2**').
- References to exhibits should be highlighted in **bold.**
- The statement should usually follow the chronological sequence of events.
- If hearsay evidence is included, the source of the information must be identified (for example, 'I was told this by my cousin, Roger Bailey, who was present at the time and who I believe to be a reliable witness').
- Contain a Statement of Truth – 'I believe that the facts stated in this witness statement are true'.
- Be signed by the witness and dated.

As a general rule:

- **The witness statements should include** the facts necessary to support all the points in your statement of case. If they don't, you may find your opponent inviting the trial judge to discount parts of your case because there is no formal evidence to back them up.
- **It will also often be very helpful** to include a bit of background information such as a (brief) history of your relationship and/or dealings with your opponent, or your reason for taking a particular decision or course of action.

For more information about the formalities of setting out a witness statement, see also pages 87–9 (small claims track) and CPR Parts 32.8 and 32.PD 18–20.

- Evidence of previous bad behaviour by your opponent is only of value in limited circumstances. The conduct complained of must be relevant to the claim. The fact that he or she is known locally as a troublemaker will add nothing to your case. On the other hand, if you have problems with your neighbour which all started because of a disagreement over the use of a parking space, that will give the court an understanding of how the situation developed.
- **In a civil claim,** character references are of very little use to either party. The court will work on the basis that someone who may be a pillar of the local community can still be liable for damage or loss in a civil claim.

SIGNING THE STATEMENT

Once the statement is complete, your solicitor will send you a copy of it for you to approve and sign. It's important to check it carefully, looking not only for mistakes but also for whether anything important has been left out. If you have any doubts or queries, ask your solicitor. It's much easier to deal with mistakes before the statement has been sent out. The rules say that, as far as possible, a witness statement should be expressed in the words of the person making it. This means it should not contain anything that you do not understand or haven't told your solicitor.

When you sign the statement, you are confirming that the contents of the statement are true. This is not just a formality. Ultimately, your witness statement will form the basis of your cross-examination at trial and the best way to make sure that you don't get into difficulties is to ensure that the statement is as accurate as possible.

Affidavits

Most witness statements are simply signed by the person making them but sometimes the court rules require that written evidence should be in the form of an affidavit. The idea is that a sworn written statement carries more force. The contents are set out in numbered paragraphs, exactly the same as for a witness statement, but the statement is signed on oath and so will begin:

'I, Christine Barclay of 43 Hill Drive, Oxford, MAKE OATH and say as follows: ...'

The person whose affidavit it is will need to sign it in front of a solicitor. Alternatively, affidavits can be sworn at your local County Court – which has the advantage of being free.

PREPARING YOUR OWN STATEMENTS

If you are doing the case yourself, you will find some tips on how to draw up your own statements on pages 87–9. Whereas observing the formalities is an optional extra in small claims cases, in fast track and multi track claims, the court will expect the rules about witness statements to be followed. However, when you are presenting the case yourself, the judge generally will be more lenient about technical breaches of the rules. As long as they don't put your opponent at a real disadvantage, the court will usually overlook any mistakes you have made.

❝Formalities aren't vital in small claims cases, but they are elsewhere.❞

Video evidence

Either side can also ask the trial judge to look at video evidence. The video or DVD must be made available to the other party well in advance. If it exists at the time disclosure takes place, it should be included in the list. Otherwise its existence should be drawn to the attention of the court and other side at the earliest opportunity.

Videos crop up most often in personal injury claims where the defendant suspects the claimant is exaggerating his or her injuries. As they are usually taken by private investigators without the knowledge or consent of the claimant, the arrival of one on your solicitor's desk can be an unpleasant shock. Nevertheless, if the case goes to trial, the judge will want to see the film and the claimant and his or her doctor can be cross-examined about what the video shows.

Exchange of witness statements

The general rule is that there should be a simultaneous exchange of witness statements, with the parties agreeing a date in advance and sending them out at the same time.

Expert evidence

Often a case can only be resolved with the help of an expert, such as a doctor or an engineer, who is able to give an opinion on what the probable cause of a problem or medical condition is. In a personal injury claim you must attach a doctor's report to the particulars of claim and even in a road traffic or factory accident it may be necessary for an engineer to report on how the accident happened and who, if anyone, was at fault.

Expert witnesses are supposed to be completely independent. They do not work on a conditional fee basis but will need to be paid whether or not they support your case. They must state clearly in their report that they understand that their first duty is to the court. Nevertheless the reality of the situation is that experts often get a reputation for being 'pro claimant' or 'a defendant's man'.

There are strict rules about expert evidence, which mean that you cannot use an expert unless the court has given its permission. In fact, CPR Part 35.1 puts a duty on the court to restrict expert evidence to that 'which is reasonably required to resolve the proceedings'. This means that if you want to use expert evidence you will have to persuade the court that it's necessary in order for the trial judge to decide the case.

Generally speaking, the higher the value of the claim, the more likely the court is to allow the parties to get their own expert evidence, but it will only do so if expert opinion on a particular point will help to resolve the case.

It will also be necessary to get the permission of the court if you want an expert to give oral evidence at the trial.

WHEN TO INSTRUCT AN EXPERT

Deciding when to instruct an expert can be tricky. Some experts have a long waiting list and it may take months for them to report back, which can mean a delay in getting the claim to trial. On the other hand, it is obviously risky to spend money getting an expert's report before the court has given its permission.

In some types of case, such as personal injury or professional negligence claims, it is necessary to get an expert's

 For the Civil Procedure Rules relating to expert evidence, see CPR Part 35.

report right at the outset. The pre-action protocols allow for this to happen and set out what the claimant has to do in order to agree with the defendant which expert to use if it's possible to do so. In other complex or difficult cases, it may be sensible to obtain a preliminary view from an expert so that an early decision can be taken about whether the claim should be pursued or defended before the costs have started to spiral.

Otherwise, the allocation questionnaire allows each side to say whether they want to use an expert. If the directions order does not allow for experts to be used, it will be necessary to make an application to the court. If both parties can agree that expert evidence is needed, the application is more likely to be granted. However, even if both sides want to use experts, the court won't necessarily allow them to do so. It will depend on whether the district judge thinks that having expert evidence will help the trial judge to decide the case.

In a case where permission from the court to get expert evidence is not a foregone conclusion, there is nothing to stop your solicitor from making preliminary enquiries to find someone who has the right expertise and can report back in a reasonable time.

It may also be better to wait until you have received all the evidence from your opponent before getting an expert's opinion. The court timetable will usually allow for this by setting the date for the exchange of expert evidence some time after disclosure of documents and witness statements.

SINGLE JOINT EXPERTS

In a lot of cases – particularly fast track claims – the court will decide that there should be a single joint expert. The idea is that using a joint expert will save time and money in cases that are relatively straightforward. If a joint expert is ordered, the parties:

- Have to agree who to use (if they really cannot agree, the court will step in and decide).
- Share the cost of the report.
- Have to agree on the wording of the letter of instruction to the expert.
- Cannot discuss the case with the expert unless the other side is either present or agrees.
- Must send copies of all correspondence to and from the expert to the other side.
- Will not be allowed to get their own expert report unless the court gives permission – which usually it won't – especially if the reason for asking is because the joint expert has come down in favour of the other side.

If the joint expert comes down firmly in favour of one side, this will usually be enough to decide the claim. Unless there are very good reasons for challenging his or her opinion, the court is likely to accept the findings. This can be very frustrating if the joint expert supports your opponent's case. If that does happen, you will usually have very little choice but to try to settle the claim on the best terms possible, but obviously you will not be in a very strong bargaining position.

What sort of expert do I need?

Claim	Expert
Boundary dispute	● Surveyor
Dispute over a will	● Doctor – if doubts have been raised about the capacity of the person who made the will ● Graphologist – if doubts have been raised about whether the signature is genuine
Housing disrepair or building defects	● Surveyor
Medical negligence	● Consultant who practises in same field as the doctor who treated the claimant ● Consultant who can give an opinion on whether the claimant's condition was caused by the treatment or by the original condition
Noise nuisance	● Environmental health officer
Partnership dispute or financial loss (a company or someone who is self-employed)	● Accountant
Pension loss	● Actuary

Personal injury	● Doctor or consultant specialising in each type of injury suffered
	● For severe injuries:
	  – Care expert
	  – Occupational therapist
	  – Physiotherapist
	  – Employment consultant

Professional negligence	● A senior member of the same profession as the person who it is alleged was negligent
Road or factory accident	● Engineer

CHOOSING AN EXPERT

Your solicitor will probably have worked with a number of experts on previous cases and may have an idea of who would be best qualified to prepare a report for you. However, the choice of an expert is something you should be able to discuss and have some input into. These are some of the things you might want to take into account:

- If you need to attend a consultation, would you prefer to go to someone based near to where you live?
- Do you need an expert with expertise in a particular aspect of their field? For example, an orthopaedic surgeon specialising in knees may not be the best person to report on a complex back injury.
- Cost: experts cannot work on a conditional fee basis, so you will need to know what the fee is likely to be and whether you will have to pay it if you lose the case.

As a general rule, you should avoid using someone who is directly involved in helping you deal with the situation. You may have a good relationship with the consultant treating you for an injury caused in an accident at work or with the architect you've called in to deal with the mess left by your builders, but it is much better to keep that working relationship completely separate from the court case. Apart from anything else, they will be open to the accusation that they are not sufficiently independent.

It goes without saying that someone you know personally, however well qualified they may be, is unlikely to be regarded by the court as entirely independent.

FINDING AN EXPERT

If you need to find an expert yourself, there are a number of directories that list experts by their field of expertise and location (see box, below). It is always a good idea to make a preliminary telephone call to check:

- Qualifications and expertise.
- Provisional cost.
- Time scale for producing a report.
- How many court cases the expert has been asked to prepare reports for over the last year and how many of them were for claimants/defendants.
- Whether, on the facts of your particular case, the expert thinks he or she might be able to help.
- If you can obtain an informal preliminary view from the expert on the merits of your case, it may save problems in the future. However, no expert will commit him- or herself finally until he or she has had access to all the information.

 Online expert witness directories include: Expert Witness Directory of England and Wales (www.legalhub.co.uk); Expert Search (www.ExpertSearch.co.uk) and X.Pro (www.xproexperts.co.uk).

DEALING WITH YOUR OPPONENT'S EXPERT

If the court agrees that each party needs its own expert, you will be expected to co-operate with the expert that your opponent has chosen to report on the claim. This may mean travelling to see him or her, or allowing the expert to come to your home or business premises to talk to you or inspect any damage. It will also mean letting the expert have access to any relevant documents. This can feel very intrusive and it can be difficult to believe that someone is approaching the claim in an impartial manner, when you know that your opponent has chosen that particular person in the hope that he or she will be able to undermine your case. However, this is all the more reason to be as pleasant and reasonable as you possibly can in any dealings that you have with the expert.

Most experts really will approach the task of preparing a report in as professional and objective a manner as possible and you should regard their involvement as an opportunity to explain your position to someone whose opinion may influence both your opponent and, ultimately, the court.

If you do encounter hostile questioning or an openly sceptical attitude, stay calm and polite and report back to your solicitor afterwards. If the hostility you have experienced does feed back into the report, there is a good chance that you will be able to show bias if the case ever comes to trial.

On a practical note, any out-of-pocket expenses that you incur as a result of attending your opponent's expert should be reimbursed.

THE REPORT

The arrival of the report from your expert (or that of your opponent) can be a turning point in your case. The report should:

- List details of the expert's qualifications, experience and any books or papers he or she has published in their field.
- Confirm that he or she understands that their primary duty is to the court.
- Set out the facts of the case, identifying the sources of information.
- Record the findings of any examination or inspection he or she has carried out.
- Discuss the issues that the claim raises, referring, where necessary, to any publications or research that helps to explain the arguments.
- Set out the conclusions that he or she has reached.

A good expert's report will make technical and specialist knowledge readily understandable to someone with no previous experience of that field. You should also be able to understand the reasons for and the evidence available to support any opinions expressed in the conclusion.

" Meeting opposition experts is a chance to explain your position. "

Ask the expert

Since the new extension was completed on our house two years ago, we've had three really bad floods with water running through the ground floor of the building causing thousands of pounds worth of damage and making it virtually impossible to sell. Our surveyor says the problem has been caused by inadequate damp proofing by the builders so we've issued court proceedings. The builder claims that the flooding happened because the local authority didn't clear out the culverts on the road beside the house so that every time there was heavy rain the water came in. The defendants persuaded the court to allow them to get their own expert report. Their surveyor came round over two months ago. He seemed very reasonable and, in fact, we got on quite well. Since then we've been waiting to see his report. The deadline for expert reports has passed and the solicitor for the other side has now announced that she is not going to use expert evidence. I presume this is because her surveyor agrees with ours. Can we insist on seeing the report? And won't the defendants be misleading the court if they try to conceal the fact that even their own surveyor didn't support their case?

The defendants commissioned and paid for their expert report and they are free to do what they want with it. This includes not disclosing it to you or the court. Theoretically you could approach their surveyor and commission him to prepare a report for you, which you would pay for. However, you would need the permission of the court to use it and as you already have a surveyor's report that supports your claim, it is unlikely that you would get it. In any case, you are already in a very strong position and don't really need to involve their surveyor further. As matters stand, the only expert evidence available supports your claim; and the defendants are not really in a position to contradict it. This gives you such a strong tactical advantage that the chances are that the defendants will want to negotiate a settlement rather than risk going to trial.

DEALING WITH AN ADVERSE REPORT

In a claim where a great deal rests on expert evidence, receiving a report from your expert or the joint expert that does not support your case is always going to have serious consequences. You may have to rethink completely how far you will be able to go.

A report may be generally helpful but reach adverse conclusions on one or two points. For example, if you are the claimant, the report may agree that you have suffered loss as a result of the defendant's actions, but that some of the claims you are making cannot be justified. If that happens, you will probably have to adjust your claim to reflect the expert's findings and that may, in turn, lead to scope for negotiating a settlement that both sides can live with.

The more difficult situation is where you are on the receiving end of expert evidence, which has the effect of completely undermining your case. If the expert was jointly instructed, even if you suspect bias, there may be very little that you can do about it.

With a joint report, one side or the other is almost certain to be disappointed. The court is likely to be very sceptical about any request to get further expert evidence in those circumstances. You can be sure that the party whose position has been vindicated by the joint expert will resist any suggestion that the report was unfair or that further expert opinion should be obtained.

> **❝ If your expert's report does not support your case, you may have to rethink how far you will be able to go. ❞**

In a case where each side has permission to use their own experts, an adverse report will also cause problems. If the report forms part of the preliminary investigation by your solicitor it may be enough to stop the claim being funded by a CFA or legal aid. If the court action is well established when the report comes through, it puts you at a tactical disadvantage because unless and until you can produce an expert's report that supports your position, you will remain vulnerable to losing the case at trial with the result that your negotiating position is immediately weakened.

WRITTEN QUESTIONS

One way of challenging an expert's opinion is to put written questions about the report.

If you are putting questions to your own expert, you can ask whatever you want, whenever you want. However, a direct challenge to their opinion or professional expertise is likely to be counterproductive. Any questions will need to be carefully phrased and based on a careful reading of the report and understanding of the reasoning behind it.

CPR Part 35.6 allows written questions to be put to a single joint expert or your opponent's expert. The directions order will usually set a deadline both for the questions and the replies. Otherwise they must be sent within 28 days of receiving the report. Strictly speaking, you are only allowed to ask questions once and for the purpose of 'clarification'. In practice, written questions are often used to try to get the expert concerned to come down in favour of the party putting them. What you cannot do is conduct an ongoing cross-examination by letter.

Although the expert concerned may be willing to acknowledge any factual errors or enlarge upon the reasons for coming to a particular conclusion; it is extremely unlikely that they will change their opinion about their main findings in response to written questions. To do so would suggest a lack of confidence in their professional opinion.

❝Opponents' experts are unlikely to change their main findings in response to written questions unless they reveal factual errors. ❞

SHOPPING AROUND

Another option is to try to obtain a second opinion from another expert. However, this is not straightforward:

- **There is no guarantee** that a second expert will support your case. Indeed, the fact that the original expert felt unable to come down in your favour suggests that it may be difficult to find someone who will.
- **If you are still in the preliminary stages** of investigating the claim, you will probably have to pay for the second report yourself.
- **If ultimately you win your case,** the cost of an expert report that you did not rely upon cannot be claimed from the other side.
- **If you want to obtain a second report** after a joint expert has reported back, you will need to make an application to the court. To succeed, you will have to show that there are genuine reasons for calling into question the expert's opinion.
- **If the date for exchanging expert evidence** is approaching, you may find it difficult to find someone else who can prepare a report in the time available.
- **If you want to get a second report,** the court may make it a condition that you show the first report to your opponent (see the case study, overleaf).
- **If the effect of getting another report** is to delay the trial, you will have an even greater uphill struggle persuading the court to allow you to do so.

Nevertheless, if there really are good reasons for thinking that the expert has got it wrong, you will need to go back to the court. To do this you will need to be able to show specific defects in the report, such as significant factual errors or obvious flaws in the reasoning. A general statement that the expert is biased or you found him or her hostile or difficult to deal with is unlikely to receive a sympathetic response.

Case Study Louise Ramage

Louise Ramage brought a claim against BHS after she had tripped and injured herself in one of its stores. She obtained a medical report, which she did not show to BHS, and then applied for permission to use a second medical report instead. The judge gave permission on the condition that she disclose the first report to BHS. Her appeal against this decision was dismissed. The appeal judge said that although an expert report obtained by a party to litigation did not have to be disclosed, if that party then wanted to obtain a second report, the court could impose such a condition. 'Expert shopping' should be discouraged and there was nothing wrong with requiring a party to make a choice between keeping the original report confidential and being able to use a second report.

Louise Ramage v BHS Ltd (10 July 2006) Slough County Court

66 A joint statement outlines points of agreement and disagreeement. 99

MEETINGS OF EXPERTS AND JOINT STATEMENT

In any field of expertise, there will always be grey areas where the experts disagree; but there are also likely to be things that everybody can agree about. In a claim where each party is using its own expert evidence, the court will expect the experts to get together and narrow the issues. Often the experts will know each other professionally and can give informal advice to their clients about the particular strengths and weaknesses of their opposite number.

At some point, usually not long before trial, the experts will need to agree a joint statement, setting out first the things that they can agree and, second, the points of disagreement. The joint statement provides an opportunity for your expert to persuade his opponent over to his way of viewing the case or vice versa. If one is more senior than the other, there is a real possibility (or risk, depending on where you stand) that he or she will obtain significant concessions from their opposite number. If this does happen and it's your expert who's made the concessions, you may have to ask more written questions to try to get him or her back on track.

Ultimately, expert witnesses are given every encouragement by the court to express opinions that are entirely independent of the parties. If that means it becomes necessary to reassess the chance of winning in the light of expert opinion, there is little to be gained by putting it off in the hope of a change of direction by the expert concerned.

Getting the claim to trial

This section looks at some of the things that can happen after the claim is up and running but before it gets to trial. Often it's just a matter of asking for a bit more time to get everything done, but sometimes an application can be made which potentially could completely alter how the case is presented at trial or whether the case goes to trial at all.

Organising the documents and evidence is the most important part of preparing the claim for trial. The arrangements for doing so are normally set out in the directions given by the court at the time the case is allocated to a track; but that, of course, is not the end of the story.

There are all sorts of reasons why the court may need to look at the case again. Not least if one side or the other wants to vary the directions with or without the agreement of the other party. The court itself will also want to review the claim's progress and make sure that everything is going according to plan.

" Your solicitor will probably handle a CMC without you. "

CASE MANAGEMENT CONFERENCES (CMCS)

In more complicated fast track and multi track claims, the court will arrange case management conferences. These are short hearings designed to check that everything is proceeding smoothly. The hearing is often done by telephone. CMCs give the parties a chance to sort out any differences over timing and evidence and allow the court to make any changes to the original directions that may have become necessary as the claim has progressed. If you have a solicitor, he or she will probably deal with any CMCs without needing any input from you.

INTERIM APPLICATIONS: PROCEDURE

In a straightforward case, the court allocates the claim to a track, sets a timetable and the parties get on with preparing for trial. The court expects the parties to co-operate with each other as much as possible. That means there should be a degree of flexibility on both sides and a willingness to agree to a short postponement if one side is not going to be ready for a particular deadline as long as this does not throw the whole timetable out or mean that the case won't be ready for trial by the start of the trial window.

There are some things that the parties can agree without getting the approval of the court: setting a later date for doing something as long as it does not affect the trial window; putting extra questions to an expert; and accepting a Part 36 offer after the date for doing so has passed. But if the parties really cannot agree on these or other matters, then it will be necessary to make an interim application to the court. Sometimes, even if the parties are agreed, it is necessary to get permission from the court to take some step in the proceedings that has not been allowed for under the original court directions.

Typical interim applications

Application	What is being asked for	Reasons for asking	Reasons for opposing
Transfer the claim to another court or track	That the claim should be dealt with by another court or on a different track	• The court or track proposed is better suited to the claim	• The current court/track is the best place to deal with the claim • Moving the claim would add to the costs
Extension of time	More time to complete the action required under the court's timetable	• There is a good reason why the current deadline cannot be met	• If the extension is granted, the case won't be ready for the beginning of the trial window
Specific disclosure	Disclosure of documents not included in the standard disclosure list	• There are other documents that are relevant to the claim • There are reasons for thinking that they are in the possession or control of the other side	• The documents don't exist • They've never been in my possession or control • They're not relevant to the claim • They're privileged or otherwise confidential
Permission to use expert evidence	Permission to get an expert's report over and above that already allowed by the court	• The issues the claim raises are complicated • The court will not be able to decide the case without this expert evidence • A fair trial of the issues will not be possible unless permission is given	• The value of the claim does not justify the cost of (more) expert evidence • The expert evidence already obtained is sufficient • The only reason more expert evidence is being asked for is because the current expert evidence does not support the other side's case • Obtaining another expert report will delay the trial
Permission for an expert to give oral evidence	Permission for the expert(s) to give evidence at trial	• The court will need to hear the expert(s) give oral evidence and be cross-examined to decide the case	• Any questions can be put to the expert(s) in writing • It will add unnecessary costs
Permission to amend a statement of case	Permission to change the particulars of claim or defence	• New information has come to light that casts a different perspective on the case • The changes will not delay the trial • The other side will not have any problem dealing with the proposed changes	

How to make an interim application

To make an application, you or your solicitor will need to complete an Application Notice (an N244 form obtainable either from the court office or the Ministry of Justice website (www. mod.uk) and pay a fee of £60. You must:

- **Explain clearly** the order that you would like the court to make (you or your solicitor can attach a draft of the order you want).
- **Give the reasons** or grounds why you need the order.
- **Set out (on a separate sheet of paper if necessary) the evidence** in support of your application. This really means giving a more detailed explanation of the circumstances that have prompted you to apply to the court. You can also emphasise any points in your favour, such as the fact that it won't put your opponent at a disadvantage or disturb the existing timetable.

- **Attach any documents,** such as correspondence or expert reports, which are relevant to your application. For example, if you are asking for permission to get a psychiatrist's report because the orthopaedic surgeon says there may be a psychiatric element to your back injury, you should attach the report that says this.
- **Sign a statement of truth** (see page 89 for wording).

Jargon buster

Applicant Party who makes an application

Application Formal request to the court

Discharge (an order) Cancel

Draft order Terms of an order prepared by one or both parties in the hope that the court will approve it

Interim Between the issue of proceedings and trial

Paginated Numbered pages

Personal service Arranging for documents to be handed over personally to the party concerned

Procedural Relating to steps that need to be taken to get the case ready for trial

Respondent Party on the receiving end of an application or appeal

Return date Date set by the court for a full hearing of an application

Ask the expert

Do I need to make an application at all?

Ask your opponent to agree to your request. If they will agree and you don't need the court's approval (see box, opposite) ask them to confirm their agreement in writing and take it from there.

 There is currently a pilot scheme involving nine County Courts where it is possible to make applications online. Full details, including which courts are included in the scheme, can be found on www.hmcourts-service.gov.uk.

How to make an interim application

If you are doing the case yourself and do need to make an interim application this is what you should do:

✓ Ask your opponent if he or she will agree to what you are asking for.

✓ If he or she agrees, ask your opponent to confirm this in writing otherwise it will not be binding on them.

✓ If he or she won't agree, make a formal written request, setting out exactly what you want and why; and explaining that if they still don't agree, you will make an application to the court and ask the court to order them to pay the costs of the application. Set a clear date by which, if they haven't agreed, you will make your application.

✓ If the deadline passes, allow a few more days just to make sure that they really are not going to agree, and then make your application. The application must be made to the office of the court currently dealing with the claim. If you are in any doubt which is the right court, ask.

✓ The court will send you a Notice of Hearing telling you the date and time the application will be heard. You must send a copy of the application and the Notice of Hearing to every other party just as soon as possible, so that they receive it at least three days before the hearing.

✓ At the hearing, the party making the application goes first. The district judge will listen to both sides' arguments and decide whether or not to allow the application.

✓ The judge may also give more directions if it is necessary.

✓ The judge will also decide who should pay the costs and how much they must pay.

✓ If a solicitor or barrister is going to do the application for you, you do not need to be there.

Resisting an application

If you are on the receiving end of an interim application:

- **First you need to consider whether there really are good reasons** for not agreeing to your opponent's request. If you resist an application without good reason, you may end up paying your opponent's costs, which are likely to be between £500 and £1,000. You can still agree, even after the application has been made to the court and a date has been set for the hearing.
- **If you don't agree,** you don't need to lodge any documents with the court before the hearing – although if you do want the judge to consider your evidence, you can send a statement to your opponent and the court explaining why you object.
- **If an order is made that you do not agree with** and you didn't have an opportunity to put your arguments to the court, you can make your own application to have the order varied or set aside. You must make the application within seven days of receiving the order.
- **If an order is made that you do not agree with** but you were represented or there at the hearing, you can appeal. You must do this within 14 days of the decision.

Interim applications without a hearing

Sometimes, if the application is very straightforward, the court will deal with it on the basis of the paperwork, without having a hearing. This can be a quick and cost-effective way of dealing with it where:

- **The parties are agreed** but still need the permission of the court; for example, if the start of the trial window will have to be delayed.
- **It is unlikely that the respondent** to the application will want to contest it.

If the court has made an order without your knowledge or consent, you have a week from when you receive a copy of the order to ask the court to set it aside or vary it and the court will then arrange a hearing.

Telephone hearings

It is also possible for interim applications to be dealt with by the court over the telephone. The court will make the arrangements with BT so you or your solicitor just need to be by the telephone at the time fixed for the hearing. This saves travelling and waiting around at court for a hearing, which may only take ten minutes or so.

 For a reminder as to the time limits that are imposed on both claimants and defendants, see page 68.

INTERIM INJUNCTIONS

It sometimes happens that a situation has developed which is so urgent that it simply isn't possible to wait for the claim to go through all the procedural stages to trial. If the purpose of the claim is to ask the court to make an order forbidding someone from doing something that is already causing real harm or upset, then it will be necessary to make an interim application for the court to make an immediate order or injunction.

APPLICATIONS WITH NOTICE

The normal rule is that even where an urgent application is made, the person on the receiving end is entitled to know about it in advance and have an opportunity to come to court and have his or her say. Usually the court will fix a hearing to take place within a few days and your solicitor will arrange for **personal service,** which involves getting a bailiff or process server to find the respondent and give him or her the court

---

The paperwork

For such applications as this, the court will want to see the following:

- Application notice
- Witness statement or affidavit
- Draft of the order the court is being asked to make
- Affidavit from bailiff or process server confirming the application has been served.

---

documents. It doesn't matter if the respondent tries to throw them away, just as long as the bailiff can confirm that he or she correctly identified the person involved and left the documents with them.

URGENT APPLICATIONS

In some cases, for example if you are suffering serious harassment, the application for an injunction will be made even before the court proceedings have been started and there will be no question of going through pre-action protocols or attempts to solve the matter through alternative dispute resolution. It will be enough for the person making the application to promise the court to issue the claim as soon as possible, for the court to make an order. In a real emergency, whether or not court proceedings have been issued, an application for an injunction can be made without telling the other person about the application or serving them with the court documents until after the court has dealt with the application. This is known as making an application without notice.

To make the application, either you or your solicitor need to go directly to the court during office hours or, out of office hours, make it over the telephone. The judge will want to be satisfied that it really is necessary to make the application without letting the defendant know in advance.

If an order is made, it will set an early return date for a court hearing so that the person on the receiving end of the injunction has a chance to put his or her side of the story. The injunction will have no effect until it is actually handed to (or served on) the defendant. It is up to you or your solicitor to arrange this. Usually a bailiff or process server will go and find the person concerned and give him or her the court papers, including the application and written evidence in support of it. You will have to pay for this service.

AT THE APPLICATION HEARING

The hearing is unlikely to take more than an hour or two. Unlike most interim applications, you will need to be there. If the application is contested, the judge may want to hear evidence from both parties, although as this is not the final hearing, the oral evidence will be relatively short: just enough to give the judge a flavour of the case and the people involved in it.

The purpose of the hearing is for the judge to decide whether an injunction needs to be made at what may be a very early stage in the proceedings. If the allegations made by the applicant are subsequently shown to be unfounded, the respondent will suffer the injustice of being subject to an injunction for the months that it takes to get the case to trial. On the other hand, if the applicant is undergoing real hardship as a result of the respondent's actions, he or she will need the protection of the court as soon as possible. It is up to the judge to try to balance the interests of both sides without prejudging what might happen at trial. This is known as the **balance of**

convenience or the **balance of justice**. Usually you can expect the judge to err on the side of caution. As long as there is some evidence that the respondent is causing the claimant a problem, the court is likely to make an order forbidding the respondent from acting in a particular way. The only exceptions to this are:

- **If the application is for the respondent** to take some positive step, such as demolish a wall or undertake building works.
- **If the only effect of the respondent's conduct** is to cause the claimant financial loss, which can be compensated for by an award of damages, which the defendant would be able to pay.

 The court can only grant an injunction against someone who is capable of understanding what they are required to do and what will happen if they disobey the order. If the person making your life a misery has mental health problems or a learning disability, however extreme the conduct, the court may refuse to make an order unless there is medical evidence to confirm that the respondent understands what is going on.

Undertakings in damages

If the court does agree to make an interim injunction, it will usually expect the applicant to give an undertaking in damages. This means that if at the end of the day it turns out that the injunction should not have been made, the person who asked for it agrees to pay compensation for any financial losses that have been suffered as a direct consequence of the injunction. If you have legal aid, you do not need to give an undertaking in damages; and, in most cases, where the injunction is needed to control antisocial behaviour or harassment, there is really no question of financial loss, even if the injunction is discharged later. However, where the effect of the injunction is to interrupt business or commercial activity, the undertaking in damages may have serious consequences if ultimately you lose the claim.

UNDERTAKINGS

As an alternative to an interim injunction, the respondent can offer to give an undertaking to do (or not to do) what the applicant is asking for in his or her application. An undertaking is a promise made to the court and has the same effect as an injunction. The only difference is that it is made on a voluntary basis. The court will provide a form in which the parties agree the terms of the undertaking. The respondent then signs it after the judge has explained to him or her the effect of giving the undertaking to the court.

This is a sensible way of sorting matters out. If the respondent is innocent of the accusations, it costs nothing to agree not to do something that he or she wasn't doing anyway. If the respondent is guilty of the conduct complained of and continues to cause problems, the claimant can apply to the court to commit him or her to prison in exactly the same way as if an injunction had been made. An undertaking should not be accepted in cases of violent or threatening behaviour where a power of arrest is needed.

Cross undertakings

In cases where each party is making allegations against the other, the court will encourage them to give cross undertakings. In other words, both the claimant and the defendant promise not to behave badly towards the other. If cross undertakings are not given, the court can, and often will, impose injunctions on both parties.

Power of arrest

In certain cases it is possible for the court to attach a power of arrest to the injunction. This means that if there is a breach, the police can arrest the person for it. The main types of case where a power of arrest is available are:

- Harassment.
- Situations where the parties are related, or are or have been married or living together.
- Situations where a council tenant is behaving in a violent or threatening manner.

147

Enforcing an injunction or undertaking

If the respondent does something forbidden by the injunction or undertaking, he or she will be in **breach** of it. This is regarded as **contempt of court**. The ultimate sanction for contempt of court is a prison sentence of up to two years. However, this is still not regarded as a police matter unless the injunction has a power of arrest. Otherwise the claimant must make a **committal** application to the court (see page 198).

> **"** Breaching an injunction or undertaking is regarded as contempt of court, but is not necessarily a police matter. **"**

Ask the expert

For how long does an interim injunction last?

Often an interim injunction has the effect of sorting out the dispute between the parties once and for all. The court will do everything it can to encourage this in an appropriate case, by setting a generous or flexible time limit for when the injunction expires. The judge may decide that the injunction should remain in force 'until trial or further court order'. Another alternative is to set the expiry date for six months later in the hope that by that time the situation will be sufficiently defused and no further action by the court will be needed. If it is obvious that there will have to be a trial, the injunction hearing can be used by the judge to give case management directions, including that there should be a speedy trial. If there is an ongoing problem and the deadline is about to expire, it will be necessary to come back to court to ask for it to be extended.

OTHER INTERIM APPLICATIONS

In addition to injunctions and applications dealing with getting the claim ready for trial, there are a number of other applications involving more complicated arguments and tactics, which can be made before trial (see the table, overleaf). These applications should only be made if there is a good reason for doing so. Apart from **interim payments**, they are nearly always fiercely fought by both parties. In addition, the rules for each of them are not straightforward. They require specialist preparation and presentation.

If you do want to make or resist one of these applications and you are doing the case yourself, you should give serious consideration to using a solicitor or barrister to advise and represent you. Losing the application may have serious consequences for the rest of the litigation and, in some cases, can effectively stop the case in its tracks.

If you are going to deal with the application yourself, get hold of a copy of the *White Book* and go through the relevant rules, practice directions and the footnotes with a fine-tooth comb. If this leaves you feeling confused rather than enlightened, it really is time to get help.

Costs orders on interim applications

Whenever an interim application is made, unless the parties agree between themselves who should pay, the court will have to decide which of them has to pay the costs of the hearing. Usually, the party who successfully argues either that the application should be allowed or that it should be dismissed will get their costs and the judge will assess there and then how much they are entitled to. But if the judge thinks this would not be fair, he or she can make a different order such as:

- **Costs in the case**: whoever wins at trial will be entitled to the costs of the application.
- **Costs reserved to trial:** whoever wins at trial will probably be entitled to the costs of the application, but the trial judge will have the final say.
- **No order for costs**: each side must pay their own costs of pursuing/defending the application.

❝Losing an application can effectively stop a case, so you may well now need advice from a solicitor or barrister.❞

See the box on page 16 'Accessing Practice Directions', for information on obtaining such legal reference books as the *White Book*.

Other interim applications

These are the some of the more contentious applications that might be made during the course of a civil case.

Application	What it means	Reasons for	Reasons against	Who can apply?
Freezing injunction (also known as a Mareva injunction) (CPR Part 25.1.27)	An order stopping the defendant from moving or disposing of money or other assets	• There are good reasons for thinking that the defendant is disposing of assets in order to avoid paying the claimant what he or she is entitled to	• The defendant has ample money/assets available to meet any judgment • The order would prevent him or her from carrying on his or her business	Claimant
Interim payment (CPR 25.6 and 25.7)	Immediate payment of a specified amount of the damages claimed, pending the final hearing	• Either the defendant has admitted liability or judgment has been entered and the claimant will recover a large sum of damages	• There are still significant arguments relating either to liability or the value of the claim	Claimant
Search order (also known as an Anton Piller order) (CPR Part 25.1.29)	An order allowing a search of a party's premises for specified documents or other evidence	• There are good reasons for thinking that the party concerned is deliberately concealing documents or information	• There is no reason for thinking that there has been any attempt to conceal information	Claimant or defendant
Security for costs (CPR 25.12 and 25.13)	Unless the claimant pays a specified sum of money in to court as security for the defendant's legal costs, the claim will be struck out	• The claimant will be unable to pay costs if ordered to do so • The claimant has not provided a current address • The claimant lives outside Europe	• The claimant is in a position to pay costs if necessary • The claimant has a good case that an order would stop him or her from pursuing	Defendant

Application	What it means	Reasons for	Reasons against	Who can apply?
Strike out (CPR Part 3.4)	An order striking out the whole or part of a statement of case (this can mean the entire claim or defence)	• The statement of case does not contain any reason for bringing or defending the claim • There are reasons why the claim should not be allowed to proceed • The party in question has failed to follow a court rule or order	• Any mistake in the statement of case can be put right • It would be against the overriding objective to deny the claimant (or defendant) the chance to pursue their case • Any fault can be punished by a costs order	Claimant or defendant
Summary judgment (CPR Part 24)	The court gives final judgment without having a trial	• The case is so clear cut there is no need for a trial	• There is a real prospect (as opposed to one that is totally fanciful) that the claim or defence will succeed	Claimant or defendant

Note Freezing injunction and search order applications are usually made without notice because letting the other side know in advance would probably defeat the purpose of the application. The court will then arrange an early hearing for both parties to attend and argue whether the order should have been made.

“Because letting the other side know about them could defeat their purpose, freezing injunctions and search order applications are usually made without notice being given. ”

MEETING COUNSEL IN CONFERENCE

Your solicitor may have asked a barrister to advise on your case or to draft your statement of case without you having met them. In fast track cases it is not unusual for the day of the trial to be the first time you meet him or her. Sometimes, though, it can be helpful both for you and your barrister to meet for a conference about the case. This is a private meeting between the client, the solicitor and the barrister, where tactics and any problems or offers of settlement can be freely discussed. If the barrister concerned is a QC, this meeting is known as a consultation. It can also be helpful for experts – though not joint experts – to attend the consultation.

The conference or consultation will take place either in your solicitor's office, or, more usually, at the barrister's offices or chambers. It can be arranged at any time during the course of the proceedings and, in complex cases, you may be asked to attend several such meetings before the case gets to trial.

The barrister is there to provide an objective second opinion about the case. He or she will have had experience of running similar cases and should be able to give you a realistic idea of what will happen if the case goes to trial. Some barristers can be very abrasive and seem to doubt everything you say. In essence, they are giving you a dry run and testing your evidence to make sure that you are able to cope with difficult questions. However, there should always be time at the end for you to raise any questions or concerns that you have. The barrister should give you an assessment of the risks, strengths and weaknesses of your case.

If you still feel uncomfortable with him or her at the end of the meeting, you should discuss this afterwards with your solicitor. Never feel that you have to make a decision there and then. Even if there is a tight deadline, you should feel able to go away and mull over what you have been told. You can always let your solicitor have a decision first thing the next morning.

Be prepared

To get the most out of a meeting with your counsel, you may want to spend a little time beforehand jotting down any queries that you have. You should also take a friend or partner with you if you can. This will mean that you will be able to discuss the advice that you get with someone you trust who was present at the meeting.

Jargon buster

Case management conference (CMC) Court hearing attended by all parties to sort out directions and get the claim to trial

Conference Private meeting with your barrister, solicitor and, possibly, expert witness(es)

Consultation The same as a conference but presided over by a QC

Pre-trial review Similar to a CMC but specifically for more complicated cases to make sure everything is ready for trial

Final preparations

Once all the documents and evidence have been dealt with, the claim should be just about ready for trial. The final preparations really revolve around the court gathering enough information to set a firm date for the final hearing. Once again the expectation is that the parties will co-operate with each other to ensure that there is no unnecessary delay.

PRE-TRIAL REVIEW

In complicated multi track claims it is usual for there to be a pre-trial review. This is really a case management conference that is arranged towards the end of the timetable and gives the parties a final chance to get everything in order for the trial.

PRE-TRIAL CHECKLISTS

In fast track and multi track cases, the parties have to complete a final checklist for the court. This provides the court with an update on how the claim has progressed and confirms that a trial is still needed to resolve the dispute. The court sets a date at least eight weeks before the start of the trial window for them to complete and send in a pre-trial checklist (this used to be known as a listing questionnaire). The checklist is designed to give the court the information it needs to set a firm date for the trial.

The parties have to provide the following information:

- **Directions** Have they been complied with and are any more directions needed?
- **Witnesses** How many are you calling (including yourself) and are any experts giving oral evidence? Are there any dates to avoid when anyone is unavailable?
- **Representation** Who will be presenting the case at trial and which dates would they not be available?
- **Time estimate** How long is the trial likely to take along with a timetable setting out the order of play and estimated time for witnesses and legal argument.
- **Costs estimate** Updated from the allocation questionnaire, to include costs already incurred and also an estimate of the cost.

 To read the specific rules that apply for pre-trial checklists for fast track cases, see CPR Part 28.5. For multi track cases, see CPR Part 29.6.

Even if everything has been done and there are no outstanding matters for the court to consider, it is still important to file the checklist confirming this. If the parties don't do this, the court will have no idea whether a trial is still required or whether the case has actually settled.

If neither side sends in a pre-trial checklist, the court will make an order striking out the claim unless either side puts in their checklist within three days. If only one party fails to send in their checklist, the court will list a hearing to take place at their expense.

NOTICE OF TRIAL DATE

If the trial date has not been fixed before the pre-trial checklists go out, the court will set a definite date for the final hearing based on the information – particularly everyone's availability and the time estimates – contained in the checklists. The court will then send a formal notice known as a notice of hearing to each party to notify them of the date. Once this has been done, persuading the court to change it will be very difficult.

GETTING AN ADJOURNMENT

If for some reason you or one of your witnesses will not be able to get to court on the day of the trial, you will need to inform everyone of this as soon as possible. In fact, you or your solicitor should be making an immediate application to the court to change the hearing date.

How sympathetic a reception you will get depends very much on the reasons for it. If the difficulty genuinely could not have been anticipated when the pre-trial checklists went in (perhaps because of a sudden serious illness), there will be a degree of flexibility. If, however, the problem has been caused by a failure to find out or give the court accurate information about everyone's availability, you can expect a fairly bumpy ride and you may be told simply that you will have to work with the date that has been set.

Generally speaking, the more witnesses, including experts, there are, the more difficult it will be to change the date. In a long trial, it may be a matter of arranging for a witness to give evidence out of sequence rather than changing the date altogether. Similarly, if one of the witnesses will not be available for a long time, perhaps because of bad health, the trial will probably have to go ahead without him or her.

GETTING YOUR WITNESSES TO COURT

In most cases, the people giving evidence on your behalf will be there because they want to support you. Sometimes, however, it may be difficult for them to get time off work. Occasionally they may be genuinely reluctant to come to court. If you really do need them to be there (and never forget that a reluctant witness can do a lot of damage to your case), you or your solicitor will have to arrange for the court to send them a witness summons at least a week before the trial is due to take place. A witness summons should persuade an employer that your witness really is needed at court. A witness summons can also be used to order someone to bring a particular document to court if it is relevant to the claim.

TRIAL BUNDLES

The claimant has to prepare a paginated bundle of all the documents including the particulars of claim; the defence; the court orders; witness statements; correspondence (but **not** letters relating to any negotiations), and relevant documents.

Although it is the job of the claimant to put together the bundles, the parties should try to agree what needs to go in. Usually the claimant's solicitor will prepare a draft index and the defendant's solicitor will either agree it or ask for additional items to be included. If there is a genuine dispute about whether a document should be included, it should be left out but copies prepared separately so that if the trial judge agrees, it can be added to the bundle. Unless there are very good reasons for doing so, opposing the inclusion of a document is usually futile and can be counterproductive since it draws attention to the document in a way which suggests that the party opposing its inclusion has something to hide.

The claimant will need to prepare two bundles for the court. One goes to the judge and the other is placed in the witness box for the witnesses to use when they give evidence at trial. In addition, it is necessary to prepare one, two or three bundles for each party depending on how many lawyers each side has. The court bundles should arrive at court between seven and three days before the trial starts. This gives the judge a chance to read the papers before the case starts.

Small claims track and trial bundles

The rules relating to trial bundles apply only to fast track and multi track cases. In small claims cases, it's a good idea to take copies (as well as the originals) of the documents you want to use to the final hearing in case the ones you sent to the court have gone astray or your opponent does not bring them to court.

Organising the trial bundle

Although on the face of it preparing the bundles is a pretty routine job, there is no quicker way to annoy the judge and bring chaos to the courtroom if it is not done properly. This means making sure that:

- Everything that needs to be included is there and easy to find. Use dividers to separate the different categories of document.
- There is an index at the front, which gives the page numbers.
- The page numbering in everyone's bundle is the same.
- Documents are not duplicated unnecessarily.
- Documents that are not relevant are not included.
- The bundles are neatly arranged in good quality ring binders with the case name and number clearly marked on the spine.

If you don't have a solicitor to do this for you, you could ask the defendant's solicitor to help out – although if you lose the claim, you will end up paying for the service.

Final checklist for trial

These are the things that you or your solicitor will need to think about in the final run-up to trial.

Documents

✓ Has there been standard disclosure and inspection of documents?

✓ Have all the issues relating to documents which have not been disclosed been sorted out?

✓ Have the parties agreed what documents should go into the trial bundle?

✓ If they have not agreed, which documents is there a dispute about and why?

✓ Are there enough copies of the disputed documents for everyone to have them if the judge allows them to be used?

Witnesses of fact

✓ Have all the witness statements been exchanged?

✓ Has the other side been told which witnesses will be giving oral evidence at trial?

✓ Are there any witnesses whose statements can be agreed, so that they do not need to give evidence at trial?

✓ If a witness cannot get to the trial, has a hearsay notice been served (see page 126)?

✓ Have the witnesses been informed of the time, date and place of the trial?

✓ Have the witnesses who are giving evidence at trial confirmed that they will be there? If not, is there a telephone number where they can be contacted?

✓ Is a witness summons needed for anyone?

Expert evidence

✓ Have all the reports that are being relied upon been disclosed?

✓ Have replies to any written questions been received?

✓ Have there been any developments since the original report was prepared which the expert needs to comment on?

✓ If an expert is needed to give evidence at trial, has the court given permission for him or her to give oral evidence?

✓ Have the experts had a chance to discuss the case and prepare (and sign) a joint statement setting out areas of agreement and disagreement?

✓ What day or days will the expert need to be at court?

✓ What are the expert's fees and who is responsible for paying them?

Pre-trial checklist

✓ Is there an up-to-date costs estimate?
✓ What is the timetable for the trial?
✓ Is there any other direction that the court needs to make?
✓ Has the pre-trial checklist been sent to the court in time?

Representation

✓ Who is going to present the case at trial?
✓ Does a skeleton argument need to be prepared?
✓ Who is going to represent the other side at trial?

Funding

✓ Has the insurer/Legal Services Commission given the go-ahead for the trial?

Settlement

✓ Does your chance of winning the case still look as good as when you started?
✓ Have you thought about what the effect of losing the case would be?
✓ Is there any potential for negotiating a settlement, which will avoid the cost and risk of taking the case to trial?

❝Is your chance of winning the case still good? What would be the effect of losing it? Is there any potential for agreeing a settlement?❞

SKELETON ARGUMENTS

In more complicated cases, particularly where there may be arguments on how the law should be applied to the facts of the case, the court may ask each party's representative to prepare a skeleton argument. A skeleton argument is a written outline of your case and it should include a brief summary of the main facts and all the legal arguments relied upon in support either of the claim or the defence. It is usually prepared by the barrister presenting the case, who will send a copy to the court, to your solicitor (if he or she is acting for you) and arrange to exchange them simultaneously with the barrister on the other side. Where the court has ordered skeleton arguments, the trial bundles will need to be ready in time for the barristers to use when they are preparing their skeletons.

Even if the court hasn't asked for them, the barristers may agree between themselves to do skeleton arguments so that each side can present its case most effectively.

❝ Usually prepared by a barrister, a skeleton argument is a brief summary of the main facts and legal arguments. ❞

The trial

Once all the procedural stages have been completed, the case will be listed for trial. The court will write to both parties to tell them the date set for the trial. You should have plenty of notice of where and when it is going to take place. Unless the case has already been allocated to a particular judge, at this stage you will not know which judge you are getting.

Getting your bearings

There are a number of things you can do to prepare for the trial and minimise stress on the day. Whether or not you are legally represented, much of the advice that applies to attending the hearing for a small claims case applies to fast and multi track trials (see pages 94-7). The main difference is that a fast or multi track trial is a far more formal affair.

If you are doing the case yourself, you will need to telephone the court office at about 3pm on the day before the trial is due to take place to confirm that the trial is in the list for the next day.

FINDING THE COURT

The notice of hearing from the court will give the address of the court where the trial is to take place. If you haven't been to the court before, you should make sure you know where it is (see box, below). The court will not necessarily be in the same building as the Crown Court, which is where most people – including taxi drivers – tend to head for. In some towns, the County Court is housed in more than one place, depending on whether the case is being heard by a district judge in his office or a circuit judge in a courtroom.

RECONNAISSANCE

If the trial is taking place locally, you may want to have a look at the court beforehand. Most civil trials are held in public and if you want to see how they work, you can go and watch one. The court ushers will usually be able to tell you which court has a trial going on. Once inside the court, take a seat at the back. You can come and go as you please, as long as you don't disturb the proceedings.

❝ You can go and watch a civil trial to see how they work. ❞

Use www.hmcourts-service.org to find the addresses of all the County Courts in England and Wales. There is also a photograph of each one, which can be very useful if you're not sure what you're looking for.

Doing it yourself: the litigant in person

Most people will have a lawyer to represent them at trial. If you are doing the case yourself, you should find the section on presenting a case in the small claims track helpful (page 95). For the more formal setting of the fast track or multi track claim remember:

- Your opponent's barrister may want to discuss the case with you before you go in to court. You should find that they are polite and professional in their manner towards you and there is no reason why you should not listen to what they have to say. If you start to feel uncomfortable or unsure about what is being suggested, simply explain that you would prefer to sort everything out in court with the judge present.

- In court, you will sit on the front bench next to your opponent's lawyer.

- You can have someone who is not legally qualified to help you. He or she is known as a McKenzie Friend. He or she can sit with you and give advice and support as the case goes along but he or she cannot speak on your behalf unless the judge gives permission.

- Never be afraid to ask the judge to explain what is happening.

- If you want to use a document to support your case, you must specifically refer to it. Don't assume that just because it is in the trial bundle the judge will take it into account. He or she won't unless you ask. In fact, the judge may not even have looked at it. The usual way of doing this is to introduce the document either when you or your witnesses are giving evidence or when you are cross-examining. For example, 'I wrote a letter to the defendant on 23rd March. It's on page 53 of the trial bundle',

or, 'Please look at page 53 of the trial bundle. Do you still say that I didn't give you the opportunity to come and put the problem right?'

- When you are cross-examining you must put your case to the witness. This means going through all the points of disagreement and giving the witness a chance to comment on your account of what happened. This is where leading questions (see box on page 171) come in useful. For example, 'You were very drunk when you came to my house, weren't you?'

- Make sure you deal with all the documents and evidence that either support your case or damage your opponent's before closing submissions start. You will not be allowed to refer to evidence or documents that haven't been mentioned during the course of the trial. If you're not sure whether you have covered something, at the end of giving your evidence say to the judge, 'I also want to rely on the estimate for repairs on page 67 of the bundle ...'

- Don't forget to prepare a schedule of your time and costs in putting together the case, which you should send to the court and your opponent a day or two before the trial.

- Bring proof of any financial loss that you have suffered as a result of doing the case yourself to court.

RIGHTS OF AUDIENCE

Only certain people are allowed to present the case in a civil court. They are as follows:

- **A party to the action**: either the claimant or the defendant (including a representative of a company).
- **A barrister** (also referred to as counsel). The vast majority of civil trials are conducted by barristers whose whole professional training is geared towards doing court work.
- **A solicitor** who has a qualification to appear as an advocate in the civil courts.

GETTING YOUR BEARINGS

Normally your lawyers will want to meet you and any witnesses about an hour before the trial is due to start.

On arriving at the court you should find the lists of the cases to be heard that day posted on a noticeboard near the entrance. These will tell you which court your case will be heard in and the name of the judge hearing it. You will also be able to see whether there are any other cases due to be heard that day in the same court.

Once you have found your case on the lists, head straight for the court where it is going to be heard. You will need to check in with the usher assigned to that court who will usually be hovering around

wearing a black gown and carrying a clipboard. It's the usher's job to book in both lawyers and witnesses as they arrive and, apart from recording your arrival, they can tell you whether anyone else on your side has arrived and, if so, where they are.

So what can possibly go wrong now?

If the case has been properly prepared and the parties have liaised both with each other and the court during the run up to trial, the chances are that everything will go according to plan. Nevertheless, things can sometimes go wrong. The most common hitch is if something happens that means the trial cannot go ahead after all. If this does occur, the court will try to make sure that any delay in getting the case back for trial is as short as possible. It is a good idea to ask if a new date can be set there and then so that at least you can leave court knowing when the trial will take place.

❝ Find your case on the lists and go to that court to check in with the usher, who will know who else has arrived. ❞

 The section 'Finding a solicitor' on pages 35–41 explains the differences between a solicitor and barrister as well as other forms of representation.

Last minute problems and solutions

Problem	What's going on?	What should I do?
I'm running late, so I won't get there in time.		• Let the court or your solicitor know. As long as the delay doesn't mean that there is not enough time to hear the case, no one will mind waiting for you to arrive.
The case isn't on the court lists.		• First check you are looking at the lists for the right day. If you have arrived early, that day's lists may not have been posted yet. If the case hasn't been included on the list for that day, it may mean the trial has been moved to another court or adjourned. • Go and ask at the court office (which should be clearly signposted). The staff should be able to tell you what is happening and what you should do. • Alternatively, telephone your solicitor.
At the last minute my barrister wasn't available to do the case and the barrister now doing it only got the papers at the last minute.	• This is usually because the barrister originally booked to do the case is caught up in another hearing, perhaps a trial has overrun or he or she is appearing in the Court of Appeal (which always takes priority)	• Although this can be very disconcerting, barristers are used to preparing cases at short notice. • If, having met the new barrister, you are still concerned, speak to your solicitor about it. However, unless the case is particularly complex, it is very unlikely that the judge will agree to adjourn the case just because your barrister is not available, and even if you get an adjournment you may find you have to pay the costs of the wasted day in court.
I've arrived at court only to be told that the trial is likely to be adjourned.	There are all sorts of reasons why this can happen, including: • A vital witness is ill • There's no judge available to deal with the case (perhaps another case has overrun its time estimate) • One of the parties wants to raise an entirely new argument or introduce new evidence, which the other party needs time to consider • There's not enough time for the trial to finish in the time the court has available	• If the trial can't go ahead for reasons beyond anyone's control, you will have to accept the delay. Try to make sure that a new date is set before you leave court, and ask that next time the case is given a clear start with no other cases ahead of it in the list. • If the adjournment is necessary because one side is at fault, that party should have to pay the costs of the wasted day in court. The court should make directions for the future conduct of the case to ensure that it doesn't happen again. • If the problem has arisen because of the way in which your case was prepared by your solicitor or barrister, you need to discuss with them what went wrong. If necessary, you may want to pursue a complaint or go to see another solicitor.

FINAL DISCUSSIONS

Ideally there should be a conference room where you can go to discuss the case with your lawyers. However, accommodation at court, especially in older court buildings, is often limited to a couple of rooms, which are snapped up the minute the court opens its doors. You may therefore find yourself huddled with your lawyers and witnesses in the public waiting area trying to discuss the merits of your case – not the most comfortable experience.

This will be the last opportunity you will have to talk with your barrister before the hearing starts. It may, of course, be the first time you have met and if you haven't had the opportunity to speak before, he or she will almost certainly want to go through your evidence in some detail. You will be asked to check the accuracy of your witness statement. This is not just a formality. Even at this late stage you will have the opportunity to correct any errors it contains and this may save you from being cross-examined about an apparent error or inconsistency which, in fact, is just a typing error or a minor misunderstanding by your solicitor when the statement was being drafted. Your barrister will probably take the opportunity to explain the procedure at trial and the possible outcomes.

In a fast track or straightforward case, your solicitor may not come to court for the trial. Alternatively, he or she may send someone more junior from the firm to sit with you in court. In a lengthy trial, your solicitor is likely to be there at the beginning and then call in from time to time as the case progresses to see how it is going.

COUNSEL TO COUNSEL

There are still some claims that are only settled on the day of trial when everyone is at court and the risks of litigation take on a sharper, more immediate edge. Even if the case itself cannot be settled, it may be possible to narrow the issues. It is almost inevitable that your barrister will want to discuss the case alone with his or her opponent. This can be a little unnerving. The Bar is a small world and the barristers may greet each other like long lost friends who are going off to have an amiable chat together, when what you were hoping for was more of the Rottweiler approach.

The first thing to remember is that the way they behave towards one another outside court will not necessarily be repeated once the talking is done and the case has started. Most judges expect there to be a degree of co-operation behind the scenes so that the court's time is concentrated on the areas of real disagreement between the parties. For example, in a case where liability is very much in dispute, it may be possible to agree the amount of damages to be paid if liability is established.

❝ This is your last opportunity to talk with your barrister, who will want to check your evidence for accuracy. ❞

There may also be administrative matters that need to be sorted out. For example, there may be a mistake in the figures, which needs to be corrected, or one side may want to have another document included in the trial bundle and it will be necessary to find out whether this can be agreed.

Your barrister should explain to you precisely what discussions are taking place and you should always be asked to agree to any offers or concessions before they are made to the other side.

If there are negotiations going on, your barrister will return from time to time to tell you what has been said and ask what you want to do. You may be given strong advice to accept or decline an offer, but ultimately the decision is yours.

If you reject very forceful advice from your barrister, he or she may make a note of this on the front page of the papers (which is confusingly known as the 'backsheet') and ask you to sign it to confirm that this is what you want to do. However, this is extremely rare and if the preparation for trial has been thorough and you have been properly advised throughout the case, there really should be no unpleasant surprises when you get to court.

Case Study Peter Smith

Peter Smith arrived at court for the trial of his personal injury claim to find that not only were both his and the defendant's barrister from the same chambers, but that the recorder hearing the case was also from that chambers – in fact he was the Head of Chambers. The recorder had also worked for other companies in the same group as that of the defendant. Mr Smith's barrister told him that he could ask for the case to be adjourned if he wanted, but strongly advised him against doing so. The trial went ahead and Mr Smith lost. The appeal court decided that while Mr Smith almost certainly had had a fair hearing, the recorder should have explained to Mr Smith that he was entitled to have the case heard by another judge if he wanted and that accordingly his decision to go ahead had not been made freely or in possession of all the facts. The only fair thing to do, therefore, was to have a fresh trial.

Peter Smith v Kvaener Cementation Foundations (2006) EWCA Civ 242

❝ Your barrister should always ask for your agreement to any offers or concessions that may be made. ❞

IT MIGHT BE A LONG WAIT

The fact that the case was listed for 10.30am does not mean it will start at that time if there are other matters to be dealt with in the same court. Usually the shorter cases and applications are dealt with first. The longer your case is going to take, the lower down the list it will be.

So even where the parties do not have much to say to one another there can be a lot of waiting around. You may want to bring something to read but it can be difficult to concentrate on anything much while you are waiting for your case to start. You can always go and sit in the court, which will give you a feel of the judge's approach. Like barristers, each judge has his or her own style and you can pick up quite a lot from watching how he or she deals with other matters. As long as the court is not sitting in private (and if it is, there will be a notice on the door saying so), you can go and sit at the back of the courtroom, slipping in and out as you wish.

If you prefer to remain outside, the usher will come out from time to time to let everyone know how the list is progressing and whose case will be called on next. If it's obvious that it will be some time before your case can start, the judge may send out a message releasing your case until 12 noon or even 2pm. This means you can leave the court building as long as you return for the appointed time. Otherwise, the waiting is a frustrating, but depressingly familiar, feature of life in the civil courts. In effect, you are tied to the court building without any indication of when the trial is going to begin. Not surprisingly, this does little to steady the nerves and the only consolation is that it is probably just as unnerving for your opponent.

❝The longer your case is expected to take, the lower down the list it will be, so there can be a lot of waiting around.❞

Getting started

No matter how long you may have had to wait for your case to come up, once the case has been called, everybody (including all the witnesses) will go into court.

The seating arrangements in court are as formal as for a wedding. Barristers occupy the front bench, but if Queen's Counsel are involved, the junior barristers sit behind them on the second bench, otherwise that is where you and your solicitor will be, directly behind your barrister. Witnesses, stray members of the public and press, sit at the back.

THE JUDGE

Once everyone is settled, the judge will make his (and the chances are that it will be a 'he') entrance. The civil courts are becoming less formal and it is not unusual for the judge not to wear the traditional wig and robes (which means the barristers won't either). Nevertheless, you should never underestimate the importance of the judge. In most civil trials there is no jury, so the judge not only acts as referee while the trial is in progress, but he also assesses the evidence and the legal argument and decides who has won and what that means in practical terms for the parties.

Most judges, whatever their manner in court, are extremely conscientious in their work and approach the task of assessing both fact and law with careful attention to detail. The odds are that you will get

one of these. If you do have concerns about the way in which the judge has conducted your case, you should discuss them with your barrister. However, it is likely that there will be little you can do if the judgment does not give you grounds for appeal.

> **Most judges are extremely conscientious and assess the facts and law carefully.**

HOUSEKEEPING

Once the judge has come into court the real business of the day can begin. If there are any last-minute applications, they will be dealt with first. Often it's just a matter of telling the judge what has been agreed but, if the application is opposed, the judge will have to hear arguments from both sides and make a decision before the trial can start.

If the case is a complex one, these preliminary skirmishes can take some time, but the implications for how the case is conducted can be very important. Victory at this stage, although reassuring, does not necessarily mean that the case

167

is cut and dried. It is not uncommon for a judge to agree to everything one party is asking for, precisely because he has formed an adverse view of their case and does not want to be accused of having been unfair to them if they lose.

OPENING

The claimant, who has to prove the case, gets both the first and the last word in a civil trial. This means that the claimant's barrister opens the case, explaining to the judge what the dispute is about and why the claim should succeed. If the claim is straightforward, the judge may cut matters short by saying that he has read the papers and understands what the case is about. It is a brave advocate who ignores such a broad hint to get on with it and call some live evidence. If, on the other hand, the case has only recently been allocated to this judge, he may make it clear that he has not had an opportunity to read all the papers and, in effect, ask the claimant's barrister to talk him through the case and refer him to all the important documents and legal principles.

The trial: order of play

Any applications
▼
Opening by claimant's advocate
▼
Claimant's evidence
▼
Claimant's other witnesses
▼
Claimant's experts
▼
Defendant's evidence
▼
Defendant's other witnesses
▼
Defendant's experts
▼
Defendant's closing speech
▼
Claimant's closing speech
▼
Judgment
▼
Costs and any application for permission to appeal

GIVING EVIDENCE

The judge has complete control over how the evidence is given. He can cut short the evidence or cross-examination of any witness, although this doesn't happen very often. Most judges prefer to drop not very subtle hints, such as 'I think I've got the point, Mr Brown' or, 'I'm not sure where this line of questioning is going, Miss Smith', when they want to hurry things along.

Normally the claimant will give evidence first, followed by any other witnesses of fact and then, if there are any, the claimant's experts. The same pattern is then followed by the defendant, who, except in very complex cases, is not expected to open his or her case. There may be practical reasons to change the usual running order. If, for example, a witness can only be there at a particular time or if it is decided that the experts should follow each other. These changes are usually agreed without difficulty.

Giving your evidence – the survival guide

Most people feel nervous at the prospect of giving evidence. The best way of looking at it is that giving evidence gives you the opportunity to tell your side of the story. There is no point in pretending that giving evidence in your own case is not stressful or important when it is obviously both these things. In fact, there is very little you can sensibly do to prepare for it. The impression you make on the court depends upon so many variable factors many of which are

beyond your control. The best – and most difficult – advice to follow is just to be yourself. If you try to rehearse what you want to say, you are likely either to sound stilted and artificial or else suspiciously smooth in your delivery. Generally speaking, judges respond best to a straightforward, unfussy, 'warts and all' presentation of the facts.

It's not surprising that giving evidence can be so nerve-wracking. Civil disputes arise out of the ordinary business of everyday life. When you pick up the phone to speak to a business associate, it won't necessarily occur to you that you should memorise the detail of the conversation because over four years later, when things have gone horribly wrong, you will be standing in a room full of lawyers who are busy analysing the legal effect of what was said. You may have to recall events that took place in the course of a few seconds or when you were injured or distressed and long before you had any idea that you might end up in court.

It is unlikely that you will lose your case because there are gaps in your memory and you cannot be precise about some aspect of what happened. The real damage is caused when the evidence you give at trial is different from earlier accounts you have given, especially

---

What do I call the judge?

A circuit judge or recorder is 'Your Honour'.

A High Court judge is 'My Lord' or 'My Lady'.

---

if the effect of the inconsistency is to 'improve' your case. This is why it is so important to check the accuracy of your witness statement and to avoid filling any gaps in your memory when giving your evidence with what you now think should or might have happened.

- **If you are the claimant,** you have the advantage of getting it over quickly.
- **If you are the defendant,** you will have to wait until the end of the claimant's case, but this at least will give you a chance to get the feel of the proceedings.

Either way you may be surprised at how quickly time passes when you are actually in the witness box. Usually the anticipation is much worse than the actual experience.

Swearing or affirming?

Before the questions start, you will be asked by the clerk either to swear an oath or to affirm the truth of the evidence you are about to give. You should choose whichever you feel most comfortable with. The court will have holy books for most religions, so as long as the clerk knows in advance what you want to do, there should be no difficulty in accommodating your needs.

Giving evidence: order of questions

Examination	Purpose of examination
Examination-in-chief	The witness confirms the truth of his or her witness statement and answers questions from the lawyer for the party whose case his or her evidence supports
Cross-examination	The witness answers questions put by the lawyer for the other side
Re-examination	The witness answers further questions from the lawyer whose case his or her evidence supports that deal specifically with points raised in cross-examination
Questions from the judge	The judge asks the witness any questions that he or she has about that witness's evidence
Questions arising from the judge's questions	The judge gives the lawyers a chance to ask anything that they want to clarify as a result of his or her questions to the witness

Note This order of questions applies to all witnesses, including experts and the claimant and defendant.

Examination-in-chief

Your barrister will ask you to look at your witness statement and ask you to confirm that its contents are true. This is the point at which you can correct any mistakes you may have noticed when checking the statement before coming into court. You simply refer to the paragraph containing the error and explain why it is wrong and what it should say.

If your barrister wants to ask you about anything that is not covered by your witness statement, he or she will need the judge's permission. This is usually given as long as the additional evidence is relevant. If the situation is ongoing (for example, if you are complaining of noisy neighbours or are still recovering from an injury), the judge will want to know how matters have progressed since you made your statement and there will be no difficulty in updating your evidence. However, it can be trickier if you have suddenly remembered something really important, which could and should have been included at the time the witness statement was made. You will probably be allowed to give the evidence, but then will be pressed hard in the cross-examination about why it was left out of your statement.

Giving evidence

When you are giving evidence, remember:

The judge will be taking a note of your evidence – either by hand or using a laptop. Without slowing to dictation pace, you should try to make sure that you do not speak so quickly that he cannot keep up with you.

Always try to direct your answers to the judge. This is more difficult than it sounds because the questions will be coming from the advocates who are standing across the room from him. In normal conversation when we reply to a question, we look at the person who asked it. It may take a conscious effort to turn towards the judge while you're speaking. However, he or she is the one person in the room with whom you need to establish a rapport and you are more likely to do this if you look at him or her while speaking.

Leading questions

A leading question is a question designed to prompt you into giving a particular answer, such as 'Did you receive the documents on March 25th?' or 'Are you still having terrible headaches?' Your barrister is not allowed to ask you leading questions. They would have to be rephrased as 'When did you receive the documents?' or 'What symptoms do you have now?' However the barrister for the other side can, and probably will, ask you all sorts of leading questions designed to get you to agree with his client's version of events.

Cross-examination

Once your barrister has finished the examination-in-chief, he or she will sit down and the other barrister (or barristers if there is more than one other party to the claim) will then cross-examine you.

It is worth remembering at the outset that it is his or her job to test your evidence and that as long as you have given a consistent and straightforward account of events you should not get into real difficulty.

Second, this is a civil, not criminal, trial. The questioning should be at least superficially polite. The judge will not respond favourably to the prolonged harassment of a witness. The barristers will know this and should behave accordingly. If you are particularly vulnerable because of age or ill health or because you have undergone some very traumatic experience, the barrister cross-examining you will know that to be anything other than sympathetic or considerate of your feelings will be totally counterproductive. Nevertheless, the whole purpose of the exercise is to try to find weaknesses in your case and you will need to weigh your answers carefully.

Re-examination

At the end of the cross-examination, your barrister has the right to put further questions to you in re-examination. Re-examination is limited to matters that were put to you in cross-examination. Any attempt to introduce fresh evidence at this stage is likely to be blocked by the judge.

Judge's questions

When your barrister has completed any re-examination, the judge may have some questions for you. It is unusual for the judge to have more than one or two questions to put, but they can be very revealing of his assessment of your evidence. If the questions refer back to a point where you were in some difficulty and provide you with the opportunity to put matters in a more positive light, this is obviously a good sign. On the other hand, if the questioning centres on parts of your evidence where you were being pressed to 'answer the question please', it probably means that you still have not provided a satisfactory answer.

It's good to talk

If the trial is adjourned for lunch or overnight while you are in the middle of giving your evidence, you cannot speak either to your lawyers or any witnesses who are going to give evidence on your behalf. This is just one of the many reasons for bringing a good friend or partner who is not involved in the proceedings to court with you. Otherwise you will have no one to discuss how the trial is going or to have lunch with, if you are in the witness box when the court breaks.

" Weigh your answers carefully when under cross-examination. "

Cross-examination: points to remember

✓ Try to remain polite at all times – however provocative the questions are. If a question is improper, your barrister will challenge it on your behalf. As long as he or she remains sitting down you should try to answer whatever you are asked.

✓ Keep your answers short and to the point. A simple 'yes' or 'no' is often all that you need to say.

✓ Do not try to work out where the line of questioning is leading. We have all watched courtroom dramas where the witness answers a series of apparently innocuous questions only to be led gently and inexorably to the kill. You will have your work cut out simply dealing with each question as it comes, without trying to second-guess the reason for asking it. Usually the questions will be as straightforward as they seem. Even if they are designed to trip you up, a suspicious reaction will only give the impression that you have something to hide. It is much better to appear open and untroubled by the line of questioning.

✓ Listen to the question. Don't jump in before the end, even if you think you know where it's leading.

✓ Answer the question. If you try to hedge around what you are being asked, you will appear evasive or, if you persist, obstructive, which will alienate the judge. If the judge starts to intervene by rephrasing the question, it usually means that he thinks the question is important enough to require an answer and he is giving you a second opportunity to deal with it.

✓ If you are asked a question that identifies or highlights a weakness in your case, make the concession quickly and with the minimum of fuss. You will almost certainly have to concede it eventually. If you try to stall, the barrister who is cross-examining you will not let it drop and will be able to use your reluctance to concede the point to argue that your are an evasive and unreliable witness.

✓ Never be afraid to say, 'I don't know' or 'I can't remember'. Judges understand that no one has perfect recall of every detail concerning their case.

✓ If you don't understand the question, say so and get it repeated to you.

✓ If you don't know the answer to a question, don't try to fill the gap with what you think the answer might or ought to be.

✓ Make it clear if you're not entirely sure about something: 'I think I only saw him twice after that', or 'It might have been the Thursday but I can't be absolutely sure.'

CLOSING SUBMISSIONS

Once all the evidence has been heard, each side makes its closing submissions. The defendant goes first. This gives the claimant an opportunity to answer any points raised by his or her opponent in the closing speech. The defendant does not usually have a right of reply although in exceptional circumstances, where, for example, the claimant's counsel raises an entirely new argument, he or she may ask for permission to respond.

Some judges sit impassively through the submissions and give nothing away. Others may intend to but, in fact, cannot help nodding their agreement with the advocate who is advancing the arguments that accord with their own view of the case. Sometimes, closing speeches become more of a debate, with the judge intervening to challenge or question the barristers. These exchanges between the judge and the barrister arguing his or her case can become heated (not a good sign if it's your barrister who's involved), but probably worse are the icy, terse interventions of a judge who has already made up his mind and is becoming increasingly bored by the attempts of the losing party to change it.

JUDGMENT

Normally, the judge will give his or her judgment immediately. Occasionally, if it is late in the day or the case is not straightforward, he or she will reserve judgment and deliver it either orally or in written form at a later date. This further delay is a miserable experience for everyone concerned. You have come to court at the end of a long and stressful process expecting that finally a decision will be made, only to be sent away again while the judge makes up his or her mind. To make matters worse, there is nothing more that anyone can do other than wait.

Although some judges in this situation will fix the date on which they intend to give judgment, it is more common for the parties to be notified two or three weeks later, when judgment will be given. Some judges compromise by telling the parties which side has won but reserving the judgment which sets out their reasoning in full to a later date.

PERMISSION TO APPEAL

If the losing party wants to consider an appeal, it is usual to ask for permission to appeal from the trial judge. However, unless the case raised some difficult legal point, the application will almost certainly be refused. This is perfectly logical since to give permission for an appeal would suggest that the judge is not sure that he or she has come to the right decision. Normally the application is little more than a formality and the fact that the trial judge has refused permission does not stop the losing party from pursuing an appeal.

 For more information on pursuing an appeal, see pages 182–91.

Awarding costs

Often the most fiercely argued part of the proceedings is after judgment has been given and the judge moves on to consider which party must pay the costs of the court action.

If you have been awarded damages, unless you also get all your legal costs, a large chunk of the money is likely to disappear in legal fees. On the other hand, if you've just lost the case, damage limitation will be uppermost in the minds of your lawyers. Reducing the amount of legal costs that have to be paid on top of any award of damages is an effective way of retrieving something from what might otherwise be a fairly disastrous situation.

The normal rule is that costs follow the event. This means that the loser pays the winner's legal costs. However, the judge can make a different order if he or she thinks it would be unfair to make the losing party pay everything, including an order that one side or the other should pay:

- A particular proportion of the costs.
- A fixed amount.
- The costs from or up to a certain date.
- Costs relating to particular steps taken during the proceedings.
- Costs relating to a distinct part of the claim or defence.

❝ The normal rule is that the loser pays the winner's legal costs unless it would be unfair to make the losing party pay everything. ❞

Factors that are taken into account

- Whether there has been a Part 36 or other offer of settlement, which the winning side has not beaten or has only just beaten.
- Whether the winning party succeeded with all or just part of his or her case.
- Whether any time was taken up dealing with arguments that really shouldn't have been pursued.
- Whether the pre-action protocol was followed.
- Whether the claimant, if he or she has won, exaggerated the value of the claim.
- The manner in which the claim was pursued or defended by the winning party and whether they have acted unreasonably, for example, by refusing alternate dispute resolution.

 For the Civil Procedure Rules relating to awarding costs, see CPR Parts 44, 45, 46 and 48.

The judge can also decide that there should be no order for costs. This means that each side pays their own costs. The judge will also decide how costs should be distributed in cases where there are more than two parties or where there has been both a claim and a counterclaim. The judge's decision is usually final and it is almost impossible to appeal against successfully unless he or she was very obviously wrong.

The one thing the judge cannot take into account is whether or not the losing party can afford to pay costs or whether ordering them to do so would cause great hardship.

Case Study Hooper v Biddle

The claimants initially alleged that they had suffered losses of £3.75 million as a result of their solicitor's negligence. Eventually they issued proceedings. By now the claim had reduced to £350,000. A joint expert then prepared a report assessing any loss the claimants might have suffered at £38,000. The claimant did not accept this and challenged the expert's opinion. Various Part 36 offers and suggestions of mediation failed to resolve the claim, until just before trial when the claimant decided to accept an offer of £38,000 on the basis that the court would decide what costs order was appropriate.

By now, each side had a bill for costs of around £120,000. The judge rejected the claimants' argument that they were the winners and therefore entitled to their legal costs. She said that the claimants had obviously exaggerated the value of their claim and that recovering 10 per cent of the amount claimed (not to mention the original £3.75 million) could not be regarded as winning. The judge therefore decided that there should be no order for costs with the effect that the claimants would be out of pocket.

Hooper v Biddle (2006) EWHC 2993 (ch)

If you have changed track, this also has cost implications – see page 104 for a resumé of these.

CALCULATING THE COST

Costs are usually calculated on the standard basis. This means:

- The amount awarded should be **proportionate** to the value or importance of the claim.
- **Any doubt** as to whether the amount claimed for a particular item is reasonable will be resolved in favour of the party who has to pay.

Alternatively, if the judge wishes to show particular disapproval of the way in which the losing side has behaved, he or she can make an order for costs to be assessed on an **indemnity basis**. If this happens, the winner is not entitled to more costs than have actually been incurred, but any doubt about whether those costs are reasonable will be resolved in favour of the party in whose favour the order has been made.

Summary assessment of costs

In fast track cases, the judge will usually decide the amount of costs the losing side must pay immediately after giving judgment. The amount awarded is based on the schedule of costs prepared by the successful party and the amounts fixed for fast track claims under the CPR plus other expenses or disbursements, such as court fees. If the successful party's costs were funded by a CFA, the judge will also decide what the success fee should be and whether the full cost of the insurance premium can be recovered.

Jargon buster

Indemnity costs Costs assessed on the basis that the benefit of any doubt about what is fair should be given to the person receiving them

Standard costs Costs assessed on the basis that the benefit of any doubt about what is fair should be given to the paying party

Summary assessment of costs Where the amount of costs to be paid is decided at the hearing

The trial

❝ A judge wishing to show disapproval of the way a losing side has behaved can order costs to be assessed on an indemnity basis, which favours the other party. ❞

Fast track trial costs

Value of claim	Advocate's fee
Up to £3,000	£350
£3,000–£10,000	£500
More than £10,000	£750

Note: If it was necessary for a solicitor's representative to be at the trial as well, an additional £250 can be claimed.

Case Study — Mary Abrew

Mary Abrew recovered damages of £3,500 after she slipped in a Tesco store. She had entered a CFA under which she paid £829 for after the event insurance and her solicitor was to get a 100 per cent success fee. The court reduced the success fee to 50 per cent and allowed £600 towards the insurance premium. This resulted in a reduction in costs from the £8,882 claimed on her behalf to £4,862.47. Tesco still wasn't happy and appealed against the decision, arguing that the success fee and the premium were still too high. The court agreed that insurance premiums in similar cases were available for £250–£350 and further reduced the amount allowed to £400, but the 50 per cent success fee was allowed. The judge said the case was not a straightforward road accident (where the maximum success fee allowed is 20 per cent) and that, at the time the success fee was set, there was enough uncertainty about the outcome of the case to justify a 50 per cent success fee.

Mary Abrew v Tesco Stores (16 May 2003) Supreme Court Costs Office

Detailed assessment of costs

In multi track claims or trials lasting longer than a day, the judge will order a detailed assessment of costs, which means the amount to be paid will be decided by a district judge or master at a later date, unless it can be agreed by the parties themselves. If there is going to be a detailed assessment, the judge may order the losing side to make an immediate payment on account based on a proportion of the costs that the winning party is claiming.

If the amount of costs cannot be agreed, it will be necessary to have a hearing. The cost of this hearing is usually paid for by the losing side. However, it is possible for the paying party to make an offer of settlement similar to a Part 36 offer, so that if the receiving party recovers a lower amount, they have to pay for the costs of coming back to court.

> **" The judge may order the losing side to made an immediate payment on account. "**

 For the Civil Procedure Rules relating to detailed assessment of costs, see CPR Part 47.

LITIGANTS IN PERSON AND COSTS

There are special rules governing how much litigants in person who have been awarded costs can claim for the time and expense that is spent preparing and presenting the case. In particular, a litigant in person can:

A successful litigant in person can also claim the cost of getting expert help with his or her costs claim as a disbursement (see Legal Costs Draftsmen, overleaf).

- **Claim the cost of disbursements** (any fees they have paid for professional help from experts or lawyers). Proof of payment is required and the amount has to be reasonable – the court will generally have an idea of what the going rate is for legal and professional services.
- **Recover any financial loss suffered** as a result of having to prepare the case (for example, loss of earnings) as long as there is documentary proof of the loss.
- **If there is no proof of actual loss suffered,** the litigant in person is entitled to be paid for the time he or she spent working on the case. This is calculated as the number of hours reasonably needed to do the work (the court will accept that it takes longer if you are not a lawyer) at an hourly rate, which is £9.25 (2007).

The amount of costs a litigant in person can claim is limited to two-thirds of the amount a solicitor would charge for the same work.

> **❝There are rules to how much successful litigants in person can claim for time and expense, limited to two-thirds of what a solicitor would charge.❞**

For the Civil Procedure Rules relating to litigants in person and costs, see CPR Part 48.6.

LEGAL COSTS DRAFTSMEN

If you are on the receiving end of a costs order in a lengthy or complex case, you may want to employ a costs draftsman to go through your opponent's schedule of costs in detail in order to reduce it, and, if necessary, represent you at any costs assessment.

In many cases, costs draftsmen can achieve a significant reduction in the bill. If you are legally represented, this is something you can discuss with your solicitor. Costs draftsmen can also help in disputes between solicitors and clients regarding fees.

Costs draftsmen and rights of audience

Costs draftsmen do not have rights of audience, so if you are a litigant in person, you cannot send one to a costs assessment hearing on your behalf. However, you can ask him or her to attend the hearing with you as a McKenzie Friend. If you do have a solicitor, he or she can also arrange for the costs draftsman to attend as their agent.

❝ In many cases, a costs draftsman can significantly reduce the bill by going through the opponent's schedule. **❞**

Jargon buster

McKenzie Friend A person who is not a lawyer but is allowed by the court to help a litigant in person present their case to the court

 To find a costs draftsman go to the Association of Legal Costs Draftsmen website, www.alcd.org.uk where there is a list of members that you can search through by town. Members have to abide by the association's code of conduct (also to be found on the website).

Winners and losers

The end of the trial is usually in every meaningful
sense the end of the case. There may be loose ends
that need to be tied up with your solicitor, but these
will be to do with the practical arrangements for
sorting out payment or costs. Unless there is an
appeal or there are difficulties enforcing the
judgment, it is time to put the litigation behind you.
If, on the other hand, the judge has
found against you, you'll need
to consider what the
implications of losing the
case are.

Losing the case

For the losing party, losing a case is inevitably more complicated and difficult, particularly if the judge's findings of fact do not accord with what actually happened. Judges are not infallible and even the most careful judge can get it wrong. Your barrister should be able to give you some insight into why you lost, highlighting weaknesses in the evidence or explaining why you did not win the legal arguments.

Unless, however, he or she is advising you that there are grounds for appeal, there is no scope for challenging the decision and ultimately you are going to have to accept defeat as gracefully as possible. This will include complying with the terms of any order the judge has made. If this involves the payment of money and you are insured, then you won't have to worry about this too much.

If, however, there is an order forbidding you from doing something or requiring you to take some positive action, the responsibility for obeying the order is yours and any failure to do what is required may lead to an application to commit you to prison.

If you have been properly advised beforehand about the risks of going to trial, defeat should be easier to come to terms with, but the reality of losing the case is something that few people feel prepared for. However pessimistic the advice given, most people cling to the hope that things will go their way. The realisation that they have lost and that

there is no scope for pursuing the case further may take some time to absorb and accept.

CAN I APPEAL?

The civil appeal system is deliberately designed to put people off from appealing against the decision of the trial judge. This is because the courts want to make sure that in most cases the final hearing really is final. If you have lost, the chances are that you are going to have to learn to live with it. If you want to appeal, you need permission from the appeal court and even if you get it, pursuing an appeal is expensive, time consuming and risky. If the claim was funded by a CFA, the insurer will almost certainly not want to take the case any further.

An appeal is not a re-hearing. All the appeal court can do is review the original decision to make sure that the judge looked at the evidence and the law in the right way. Only in very exceptional circumstances will it hear evidence from live witnesses or consider fresh evidence that wasn't used in the original hearing.

You have 14 days from the date of the judgment to make your application for permission to appeal. If you are late making the application, you can ask for an extension of time, but unless there is a good reason for not being able to get the application in on time, you are unlikely to get it.

GROUNDS FOR APPEAL

The appeal court will always proceed on the basis that the trial judge is the person who was in the best position to decide the claim. He or she is the one who has watched the witnesses giving their evidence, watched them react to cross-examination and been able to evaluate their evidence in a way that the appeal court cannot. This means that the decision will only be overturned

What can the appeal court do?

- Overturn or set aside a judgment or decision.
- Vary a court order. For example, it may uphold a finding on liability but reduce the amount of damages awarded.
- Dismiss an appeal and affirm the judgment or order that has been made.
- Order a new trial.
- Send the case back to the judge whose decision is being appealed for a particular point to be reconsidered or decided.
- Vary or make an order for costs.

if it is obvious from the judgment that the trial judge got it wrong (see box, below).

If you are considering an appeal, you really do need to take legal advice.

Reasons for appealing

The main reasons you might be able to appeal are if the judge:

- Failed to take into account an important piece of evidence.
- Made an important finding of fact when there wasn't any evidence to support it.
- Failed to explain why he or she accepted the evidence of one witness and/or rejected the evidence of another.
- Took into account something that was irrelevant which affected the final decision.
- Taking all the evidence together, reached a decision that was so perverse that no reasonable judge could have done so.
- Got the law wrong.
- Refused to allow important evidence to be given.
- Allowed last-minute evidence or arguments to be heard without giving the other side a chance to consider or investigate them.
- Conducted the hearing in a way that was unfair to one side.
- Failed to follow a decision made by a higher court, which set guidelines on the law or on procedure.

- **If you did the case yourself,** you need to find a solicitor specialising in the area of law relating to your claim as soon as possible (see pages 35–41).
- **If you already have legal representation,** you can ask your barrister at the end of the hearing whether he or she thinks there is any point in trying to appeal. If the answer is no, you probably cannot take it any further. If you feel very strongly that you have a good reason to challenge the judgment, you may want to consider getting a second opinion from another barrister. Your solicitor should be able to arrange this for you, but it will need to be done quickly if you are to meet the 14-day deadline.

If you are told that there may be reasons for challenging the decision, you should leave it a day or two to let the dust settle (but not much longer since time is short) and then if you still want to consider an appeal, speak to your solicitor. At this stage it is a good idea to go back to your barrister to ask their considered opinion. Your solicitor can either discuss it on the telephone with your barrister or ask him or her to prepare a written advice setting out why they think the judge got it wrong and what the chances are that an appeal would succeed.

At this stage, the cost will be relatively low because the application for permission to appeal does not involve your opponent and is dealt with by the appeal court without a hearing. Your solicitor will have to send all the documents (see table, opposite) in to the court and the court will notify you a few weeks later whether or not you have been given permission to appeal.

Where to appeal

Not all appeals go to the Court of Appeal. It will depend on the type of hearing and the level of judge who heard the case.

Type of hearing	Judge who heard the case	Where to appeal
County Court: interim application	District judge	Circuit judge
County Court: interim application	Circuit judge	High Court
County Court: small claims or fast track final hearing	District judge	Circuit judge
County Court: fast track final hearing	Circuit judge	High Court
County Court: multi track final hearing	District judge	Court of Appeal
County Court: multi track final hearing	Circuit judge	Court of Appeal
High Court: interim application	District judge	High Court
Any	High Court judge	Court of Appeal

Documents needed for an application for permission to appeal

Document	What it is	What it costs
Notice of appeal: Form N161 (for obtaining, see page 69)	Court application form setting out the grounds of appeal (see below) and the order you want the appeal court to make	Small claims track: £100 All other appeals: £120
Grounds of appeal	Formal reasons for appealing usually prepared by your barrister	Barrister's fee depending on the amount of work involved but usually at least £500
Transcript of judgment	If the judge has given an oral judgment, you will need to get the tapes from the court and have them transcribed. If they are not ready in time, your barrister should have made a full note of the judgment and will have to use that until the transcript is ready	The cost of a transcript will depend on the length of the judgment, but usually will cost in the region of £300–£500. If you are doing the appeal yourself and cannot afford a transcript, the court may pay for it. If the judge handed down a written judgment, you won't need to pay this
Appeal bundle	Paginated bundle of all the documents relating to the case – the trial bundle (see page 155) can be adapted for this purpose	Your solicitor's costs of preparing and photocopying it, which will depend on the amount of documents but should be between £100 and £300
Skeleton argument	Usually prepared by your barrister and puts forward more detailed written arguments as to why the judge got it wrong	Barrister's fee depending on the amount of work involved, usually at least £1,000, and often much higher
Court order	The order that is being appealed against after it has been 'sealed' (date stamped) by the court	Nothing
Any witness statement or affidavit in support of any other application you are making	If you are applying for an extension of time or stay of execution, you will need evidence to support your application	Solicitor's costs of preparation at his or her hourly rate, depending on the time it took
Transcript of the evidence	You will only need this if you want to appeal against the judge's findings on the evidence	Depending on how much of the evidence you need transcribed, this can be extremely expensive

Notes

1 VAT is added to all the lawyers' fees.
2 In appeals from the small claims track you only need to send in your appeal notice, a copy of the order you are appealing against and any documents that you think are relevant. You do not need a transcript of the judgment.

Difficult cases

There are some appeals that are particularly difficult to get permission for. They are:

- Appeals against case management decisions, which is where the judge has made a decision about the procedure for getting the claim ready for trial or how the trial was conducted.
- Appeals against costs orders.
- Second appeals, where you are trying to appeal against the decision of a High Court or circuit judge who heard your appeal from a district judge's decision.

IF PERMISSION IS GRANTED

If you get permission to appeal, you do not necessarily have to go ahead with it. It may be that by the time the reply comes from the court, you have moved on and do not want to become embroiled in further court proceedings. If that is the situation, you do not need to do anything at all except write to the court and your opponent to tell them you've decided not to take it any further. If you decide to proceed to appeal, all the documentation needs to be served on your opponent within seven days.

IF PERMISSION IS REFUSED

If the court refuses you permission to appeal, you can apply for an oral hearing. Once again your opponent will not be involved. Basically, the court will arrange a short hearing and your barrister will have a 20-minute slot to try to persuade a judge (or judges if you are in the Court of Appeal) that permission should be given after all. If permission is still refused, that will be an end of the matter. There is no further right of appeal. In some cases where the appeal is considered by the appeal judge looking at the papers to be completely hopeless, you will not be allowed an oral hearing but will just have to accept the appeal court's decision to refuse permission.

STAY OF EXECUTION

The fact that you have applied for, or even been given, permission to appeal, will not automatically prevent your opponent from enforcing a judgment or costs order against you. You can try asking him or her to wait until the appeal has been dealt with but most people will not agree to this. The only alternative is to make an application to the court for a **stay of execution**. If you succeed, the judgment will be put on hold for the time being.

It is difficult to get a stay of execution because the general rule is that a successful litigant should not have to wait any longer to receive what a judge has decided they are entitled to after a full hearing of the claim. Some people will try to use the appeal process as a delaying tactic and the courts try to discourage this by only agreeing to a stay of execution if allowing the order to be enforced might result in real injustice to the appellant.

> **❝ Permission to appeal will not automatically prevent your opponent from enforcing a judgment against you. ❞**

Doing the appeal yourself

It is very unusual, although not unheard of, for a litigant in person to undertake an appeal and succeed. If you are thinking of doing it, you need to have a realistic idea of what's involved. The main reason why it is so difficult for someone who is not legally qualified to prepare and present an appeal is because usually an appeal will only succeed if it can be shown that the judge got the law wrong. In order to attack the judge's reasoning set out in his judgment you need to be able to analyse the legal principles involved and demonstrate where the judge went wrong and how the law should have been applied. This is very specialised work, which many lawyers find difficult to do. You may also find that the appeal court gives you a less sympathetic hearing. The appeal judge or judges will be quick to cut you short if they do not think there is anything much to add to what has already been said.

What will the court take into account on an application for a stay?

- The type of claim and remedy that the court has granted.
- The financial circumstances of both parties.
- Whether the appeal has any chance of succeeding.

- Whether or not granting the stay will prevent the appellant from appealing.
- Whether the appellant has previously acted in a way that suggests the appeal might be just a delaying tactic.

 For the Civil Procedure Rules relating to stay of execution, see CPR Part 52.7.

HOW TO RESPOND TO AN APPEAL

It can be very disconcerting to find that just when you thought everything had been settled in your favour, your opponent has asked the appeal court to re-open the case. The appellant has to send you a copy of the appeal notice, but you do not need to do anything at all unless and until permission to appeal is given. If permission is granted, it is because the appeal court has decided that on the face of it, there may be a reason for challenging the judge's decision. Normally, the judge who gives permission to appeal will give a short written explanation as to why he has done so.

As most appeals fail, you are probably in a stronger position than your opponent, but it is possible that the judgment may be open to criticism. If so, you need to find out as soon as possible and you really should take legal advice. If your solicitor or barrister says that the appeal has a good chance of succeeding, you will need to discuss with them what your options are. There is nothing to stop you from trying to negotiate a settlement, including making a formal Part 36 offer, or getting the case referred to an alternative dispute resolution.

In practical terms, you or your lawyers may want to lodge a respondent's notice. This will be necessary if:

- **You also want to appeal against some part of the judge's decision** (note that you will also need permission to do this, although if permission has been given on the main appeal you are likely to get it).
- **You want to ask the appeal court to uphold the judge's decision** for another or different reasons from the ones he gave in his judgment.

The respondent's notice must be sent to the court within 14 days after the notice of appeal is received or by whatever deadline the court has set and served on the appellant within seven days of sending it to the court.

> ❝ Most appeals fail, but the judgment may be open to criticism, and you should now take legal advice and discuss what your options are. ❞

For information on a Part 36 offer, go to pages 110-15, and for alternative dispute resolution options, see pages 20-30.

Appeal timetable

Procedural step	Time for doing it
Ask for permission to appeal	At the time the judge notifies the court of his decision
Ask for permission to appeal	In writing to the appeal court within 14 days of the decision unless the court allows more time. The appeal notice and skeleton argument must also be served on the respondent within seven days of filing it with the court
Ask for permission to have an oral hearing of the application for permission to appeal	Within seven days of receiving notification from appeal court that permission has been refused
Serve the appeal documentation on the respondent	Within seven days of receiving notification from appeal court that permission to appeal has been given
Appeal court sends 'listing window' when the appeal will be heard and, in the Court of Appeal, the date by which the appeal will be heard (the 'hear by' date), as well as any other directions for the appeal	At the time permission to appeal is given
Court of Appeal sends appellant appeal questionnaire	At the same time as permission is given
Appellant sends court completed appeal questionnaire giving a time estimate for the appeal	Within 14 days of notification of permission to appeal
If respondent disagrees with the time estimate, he or she notifies the court	Within seven days of receiving the appeal questionnaire
Respondent's notice served	Within 14 days of receiving notification that permission to appeal has been given
Respondent's documents added to the appeal bundle along with the order or judgment giving permission to appeal	Once permission to appeal has been given and in good time for the hearing

Note   Normally, a case manager will be appointed to deal with the appeal and liaise with the parties

APPEALS TO A HIGH COURT OR CIRCUIT JUDGE

The hearing will take place in your local County or High Court. The judge sits alone and listens to each side's legal arguments. The appellant goes first, then the respondent with the appellant having a final right of reply. As with closing submissions at the end of a trial, the judge may interrupt the advocates to ask them to deal with a particular point. It is very different from a trial. There are no witnesses and the discussion is confined to analysing the decision that is the subject of the appeal. The judge will give his or her decision at the end unless the case is particularly complicated and the judge wants time to consider it; in which case a written judgment will be handed down soon afterwards. You will only be allowed to appeal against the decision to the Court of Appeal if the appeal raises an important point that is of general importance.

APPEALS TO THE COURT OF APPEAL

Most hearings take place with either two or three appeal judges in the Royal Courts of Justice on the Strand in London. Civil appeals tend to be heard in the annex at the back of the courts but wherever they take place, they are extremely formal. The judges will take the initiative in raising the points of argument that they think are important and are often extremely combative with the barristers as they present their case.

In most appeals by the end of the hearing it will be obvious which side has won, but the court will almost always reserve judgment with one or more of the judges preparing a written judgment which is sent to the parties' solicitors shortly before the judgment is delivered in public so that any factual errors can be corrected.

APPEALS TO THE HOUSE OF LORDS

If the Court of Appeal has ruled against you, your only option now lies in appealing to the House of Lords. Once again you need permission to go there and you will only get it in cases that raise a point of law of public importance and which could affect a lot of other people as well as you. To get permission, you

❝ You will only be allowed to appeal against a decision by the Court of Appeal if it involves a point of general importance. ❞

 Legal aid is more restricted these days – see pages 46-7 for more information on the subject.

must either persuade the Court of Appeal to grant it at the time they give judgment, or make an application to the Appeals Committee at the House of Lords. If your case genuinely does raise a point of public importance, you must get legal representation. Indeed, if you are on a low income and there is real merit in your case, you should be able to get legal aid.

Case Study   Mrs Pigford

Mrs Pigford claimed damages from Sunderland council for a serious injury to her leg after she slipped on a brick walkway in a housing estate at about 9am one winter morning. At trial it was agreed that if the surface of the walkway had been wet, the council would be liable but that if it had been icy they would not be. Various enquiries into the cause of the accident had been carried out immediately after the accident and Mrs Pigford had repeatedly said that she had slipped on ice. This was also alleged by her solicitor in the letter of claim. However, in her witness statement and when she gave her evidence at trial Mrs Pigford said that the walkway was wet. A neighbour gave evidence that the walkway was frosty and wet at the time of the accident. Weather reports showed it had been icy overnight with a thaw taking place during the morning. The judge found in Mrs Pigford's favour and the council appealed.

The appeal judges could not agree. Lord Justice Aldous thought the appeal should be allowed. He said that Mrs Pigford had not explained the contradictions in her evidence and that the first time the neighbour had been asked about the condition of the walkway was at trial, over three years after the accident and that anyway the judge had misunderstood her evidence. The other two appeal judges upheld the judgment. They said that the evidence of the neighbour, which was consistent with the weather report, was sufficient for the judge to decide that the walkway was wet. They thought the judge's finding was 'surprising' but not 'perverse'. The appeal was dismissed.

Pigford v Sunderland (2003) EWCA Civ 823

Enforcement

If you have got a judgment against a large organisation or there is an insurer in the background, you can be reasonably sure that you are going to get paid whatever the court decides you are entitled to.

It may be a different matter, however, if you have a judgment against someone on a low income or a business that's in financial difficulty. If that is the situation, you will have to consider whether to spend more time and money trying to enforce your judgment or costs order. The hard truth is that unless you have good reason for thinking that they're good for the money, it simply may not be worth the effort and expense. All the methods outlined opposite involve going through the court and paying further fees and expenses.

66 Sadly, the hard truth is that it may not be worth the effort and expense of seeking enforcement against someone who is on a low income or a business that is in financial difficulty. 99

TRANSFERRING A JUDGMENT TO ANOTHER COURT

You will need to transfer the judgment:

- From the High Court to the County Court if you want an attachment of earnings order
- From the County Court to the High Court if you want to enforce a judgment over £5,000 by selling the **judgment debtor**'s goods or if the debt is more than £600 and you want to use High Court enforcement officers to recover the money.

In either case, the court where you obtained your judgment will help you to complete the necessary paperwork.

 For the Civil Procedure Rules relating to enforcement, see CPR Part 70.

Enforcing a money judgment or costs order: the options

Method	Which court?	What it means	Who does what?
Order to obtain information from a judgment debtor (CPR Part 71)	High Court or County Court	The debtor has to come to court to answer questions about his or her finances	You need to arrange for personal service of the order and file an affidavit confirming this has been done. The questions are put by a court official (or sometimes a judge, in which case you must be there)
Writ of Fi Fa	High Court (only the High Court can deal with debts over £5,000 – see transferring the judgment, opposite)	Sale of the debtor's possessions to pay the judgment debt	High Court enforcement officers go to the debtor's premises and prepare a list of items be sold
Warrant of execution	County Court for debts between £600 and £5,000	Sale of the debtor's possessions to pay the judgment debt	Court bailiffs write to the debtor asking for payment within seven days. They then go to his or her premises to decide what should be sold
Third party debt order (CPR Part 72)	High Court or County Court	A court order requiring a third party (usually a bank or building society) to pay money owing to or held on behalf of the debtor to you	You make an application to the court. Initially an interim order is made to give the debtor and the third party a chance to be heard. The order is then either discharged or made final
Attachment of earnings	County Court	A court order that the debt is paid off by deductions from the debtor's wages, paid directly to you by the employer	You make an application to the court. If an order is made, either side can apply within 14 days for the order to be varied or set aside
Charging order (CPR Part 73)	High Court or County Court	An order using the debtor's property as security for the debt. If the debt isn't paid, the property can be sold	

Note Although you are not entitled to get more than you are actually owed, there is nothing to stop you from using more than one method of enforcing the debt at the same time.

THE COST OF ENFORCING A JUDGMENT

If you want to use any of the methods set out in the table on page 193, you need to pay a fee to the court when you make your application (see table, below).

If you decide to use the court bailiffs or High Court enforcement officers, you will also have to pay their fees. The fee scales for High Court enforcement officers are set out in the High Court Enforcement Officer Regulations 2004

&& A High Court enforcement officer or a bailiff can concentrate the mind of the debtor. 33

and are on a sliding scale depending on the amount recovered and how the money is obtained. For example, they are entitled to 10 per cent of the price of goods sold at auction in excess of £1,000. Even if you don't recover anything, you will still need to pay approximately £100–£150 for the service they provide.

BAILIFFS AND HIGH COURT ENFORCEMENT OFFICERS

The arrival of the bailiff or a High Court enforcement officer can be an effective means of concentrating the mind of the judgment debtor to pay the money owing. They will arrive (often without notice in the case of the High Court enforcement officer) and if the money is not forthcoming from the judgment debtor, they will make an inventory of any property owned by the debtor, which can be sold to help clear the debt. Either the goods are removed immediately or the debtor can enter into a **walking possession** agreement. This means that the debtor promises not to dispose of any of the goods on the inventory and that they remain in his or her possession for the time being. If it's possible to come to an agreement to pay the judgment debt by instalments the agreement won't be enforced as long as the payments continue to be made.

County Court fees	
Enforcement method	**Fee**
Order to obtain information	£45
Warrant of execution for more than £125	£55
Third party debt order	£55
Attachment of earnings	£65
Charging order	£55

The court service website – www.hmcourts-service.gov.uk – has useful leaflets that you can download on orders to obtain information, warrants of execution, attachment of earnings orders, third party debt orders and charging orders.

Case Study   Mr Edozie

Mr Edozie rented a business unit from Workspace, who issued proceedings for arrears of rent. The unit needed repairs and Mr Edozie claimed that he had reached an oral agreement with one of Workspace's employees that he would not have to pay any rent until the work was done. Workspace denied this and sent in bailiffs who took away and sold goods from the premises.

At trial Mr Edozie represented himself. The judge rejected Mr Edozie's evidence that Workspace had agreed that he should not pay rent until the premises were repaired and gave judgment for Workspace. Mr Edozie applied for permission to appeal. He argued that the trial had been unfair because the judge had not allowed him to put his case. In particular, the judge had cut short his closing submissions.

The Court of Appeal refused Mr Edozie's oral application for permission to appeal. The court held that the judge had acted correctly in stopping Mr Edozie from continuing with his closing speech because it contained evidence not argument. The proceeds of selling Mr Edozie's goods had been taken into account and there was no prospect of Mr Edozie being able to challenge the judge's finding of fact that there had been no agreement.

Workspace v Edozie (2003) EWCA Civ 1016

Jargon buster

Enforcement Ensuring that a judgment is complied with
Judgment creditor Person who is owed money under a judgment or costs order
Judgment debtor Person who owes money under a judgment or costs order

❝ The debtor's property can be removed immediately or he or she may be allowed to keep it and pay the debt by instalments. ❞

If you want to complain or obtain further information about the services the High Court enforcement officers offer, you can go to the High Court Enforcement Officers Association site at www.hceoa.org,uk.

DEALING WITH A JUDGMENT OR COSTS ORDER

If you have had a judgment or costs order made against you and are on the receiving end of enforcement proceedings, you will need all the help you can get. Remember:

- A bailiff or enforcement officer cannot come inside your house unless you agree. However, they can get access to business premises through an open door or window.
- Nothing can be taken from you to sell that:
  - You need to earn your living
  - Is an essential household item
  - You do not own (for example if you are buying it under a hire purchase agreement).

You are entitled to four days notice of any sale of your possessions:

- If you do receive an order from the court requiring you to do something, you should not ignore it. If you do, you are at risk of being found to be in contempt of court.
- If you can, try to come to an arrangement for paying the money you owe in instalments.
- If judgment was entered against you in default and you dispute that you are liable, you must apply to set aside the judgment as soon as possible.
- If you want to stop the enforcement proceedings, you will need to apply to the court as soon as possible for a stay of execution. However, you will need to put forward positive proposals for dealing with the judgment debt.

Ask the expert

Can anyone find out about the judgment?

High Court and County Court judgments are registered with the Registry Trust (www.registry-trust.org.uk). Anyone going to the website and paying a fee can search for judgments entered against you. If the full judgment debt is paid within a month, you can apply for the entry to be cancelled on payment of a fee of £15 and proof of payment. Otherwise the judgment will remain on the register for six years, although once the amount owing has been paid the entry will be amended to show that the judgment has been satisfied.

For more information on judgment debtors, go to www.hmcourts-service.gov.uk and download leaflets *Paying my judgment – What do I do?* (EX20), *I cannot pay my judgment – What can I do?* (EX326) and *Registered judgments – What does it mean?* (EX320).

- **If you find you cannot maintain payments** under an arrangement that you have made with the judgment creditor, seek immediate advice. You will need to make an application to the court to vary the agreement unless the creditor will agree to accepting reduced payments.

" If a judgment or costs order is made against you and you are on the receiving end of an enforcement order, you need all the help that you can get. **"**

 Debt counselling is available through the Citizens Advice Bureau (www.adviceguide.org.uk), the National Debtline (www.nationaldebtline.co.uk) and the Consumer Credit Counselling Service (www.cccs.co.uk). See, too, the *Which? Essential Guide* to *Managing Your Debt*.

Committal proceedings

If the court has made an injunction either ordering someone to do something or forbidding them from behaving in a particular way, and they disobey the order, they are regarded as being in contempt of court. In the last resort they can be sent to prison for up to two years.

It does not matter whether the injunction was an interim order or a final order. The important thing as far as the court is concerned is that the person concerned has ignored its order or the promise made (if an undertaking was given) and therefore must be punished. There is a range of penalties for contempt of court but the first thing that needs to be done is to get the person in breach of the injunction back before the court.

In cases where the original injunction had a power of arrest attached, this may not be a problem if the police have carried out an arrest.

However, if the police have not become involved, the party who wants to enforce the order will have to make a committal application to the court. The basis of the application is to put the person who has breached a court order in the position of having to show cause (or good reason) why he or she should not be sent to prison.

COMMITTAL APPLICATION

Any potential threat to the liberty of the individual is regarded extremely seriously by the courts. In committal proceedings in the civil courts there are stringent rules to ensure that the rights of someone who may be at risk of going to prison are safeguarded. This means that the committal application must comply with a number of detailed requirements. Their purpose is to make sure that the person on the receiving end (the respondent) understands what the consequences of disobeying a court order could be. Someone applying for a

 A power of arrest gives the police authority to arrest the person named in the injunction. For more information, see the box on page 147.

committal order must be able to show the court that:

- **The respondent was made aware** of what was required under the injunction either because they were in court at the time the order was made (or the undertaking given) or because the order containing the injunction was personally served on them.
- **The respondent was told what the consequence of disobedience could be,** either because it was explained in court by the judge or because the court order contained a written warning that if the order was not obeyed the respondent could go to prison.
- **The correct forms** for the application have been used.
- **The evidence supporting the application** is set out in an affidavit (see page 128).
- **The application to commit** has been personally served on the respondent.
- **The application sets out the precise details** of the injunction and the allegations against the respondent in enough detail to be able to understand and answer them.
- **The application contains a warning** that the respondent may be sent to prison.
- **Except in an urgent case,** the respondent has had 14 days' advance notice of the hearing.

The rules are technical and complicated. They are not contained in the CPR but come from the old High Court and County Court Rules, which can lead to confusion. The respondent will be entitled to legal aid to ensure that he or she is legally represented at the hearing. If you want to make a committal application and you have not already got a solicitor, you must consider using one now.

If it is obvious that the respondent knows perfectly well what the situation is, the court does have the power to make a committal order, even where all the rules have not been complied with, but it will give the benefit of any doubt to the respondent. This means that if you cannot satisfy the court that everything is on order on your application, it is likely to be adjourned.

❝There are stringent rules to safeguard the rights of someone at risk of going to prison, so the committal application must meet a number of requirements. ❞

THE HEARING

The application will take place in open court with the judge and barristers wearing robes and wigs. Bailiffs will probably come and sit at the back of the court in case an order sending the respondent to prison is made (if they are not there, you can take this as a sign that the judge has already decided against an immediate custodial order). The possible outcomes are:

Adjournment

Either because the paperwork is not in order or because the respondent wants to get a lawyer to represent him or her, such an application will almost certainly be granted by the judge, who may take the initiative in suggesting to the respondent that they need legal representation.

The respondent admits the breach

If this happens, your barrister will outline the facts and suggest what the punishment should be. The respondent or his or her barrister will then have the chance to put forward any mitigation (reason or circumstances which suggest the punishment should not be too severe) and the judge will decide what the appropriate penalty is.

The respondent denies the breach

If this happens, there will be, in effect, a mini-trial in which you will have to give evidence about what happened and the respondent may also give oral evidence. The judge will then decide whether the respondent has disobeyed the order and, if so, what the punishment should be. Note that unlike other civil matters, the standard of proof that applies is the criminal one of beyond reasonable doubt.

You may sometimes be faced with a situation where some of the breaches are admitted but others are denied. You will then have to decide whether the ones that have been admitted are enough, or whether you still want to try to prove the ones the respondent denies. If only minor breaches are admitted, you will probably have nothing to lose by asking the judge to hear the evidence in respect of other, more serious, incidents, but the decision will depend very much on the facts of your particular case.

PENALTIES FOR CONTEMPT OF COURT

If the breaches of the court order or undertaking are admitted or the judge finds they have been proved beyond reasonable doubt, the court must

 For advice on what to do in the case of adjournment, see 'So what can possibly go wrong now?' on page 162.

consider what punishment is appropriate. This will depend on the seriousness of the respondent's behaviour and whether this is the first time he or she has breached the court order.

The maximum sentence that can be imposed is two years in prison. However, it is very unusual for anyone to be given a sentence of more than three months and, unless there was violence or serious harassment involved, the court will not usually send someone to prison immediately, but is more likely to make a suspended order. This means that if the respondent breaches the order again, the court can activate the prison sentence as well as imposing a further punishment for the new breach. If the breach is proved, the respondent will also be ordered to pay the costs of the committal application assessed on the indemnity basis.

PURGING THE CONTEMPT

If someone has been sent to prison for being in contempt of court, they can ask to **purge** their contempt by coming back to court to apologise to the judge and promising to obey the terms of the court order in the future. If the judge believes that the apology and statement of future intention are genuine, it is likely that the person in contempt will be released.

Someone sent to prison for contempt of court is eligible for remission like any other prisoner. This means that if the sentence imposed is six months or less, he or she will serve half the time before being released.

Civil Procedure Rules (CPR)

The rules are divided in 'Parts' and the most important ones are set out in the table below. The Civil Procedure Rules and Practice Directions are set out in full on the Ministry of Justice website, www.justice.gov.uk. On the website, click 'What we do', which will take you to the site index. Click on 'Civil procedure rules' and this will take you to the page containing the rules and practice directions.

If you don't have access to the internet, you should find them in the reference section of your local library. Ask for Volume 1 of the *White Book* or the *Green Book*. These are the reference books used by civil lawyers. The rules and practice directions are set out in full and are annotated, explaining how the rules have been applied by the courts in previous cases.

CPR	Subject	What it means
Part 3	The court's case management powers	Within the proceedings, the court can make any order it thinks necessary to ensure that justice is done; including, in an extreme case, striking out the claim altogether
Part 7	How to start proceedings – the claim form	The rules for issuing and serving a claim in the civil courts
Part 15	Defence and reply	How to file a defence, a reply or a counterclaim
Part 16	Statement of case	What needs to be included in setting out your claim or defence for the court
Part 18	Requests for further information	Can be made by either party in writing at any stage; does not apply to the small claims track
Part 20	Counterclaims and other additional claims	What to do if you are defending a claim and wish to either counterclaim against the claimant or add another party to the proceedings because what happened was their fault

> **"Volume 1 of the *White Book* or the *Green Book* set out the CPR and Practice Directions in full with annotations."**

CPR	Subject	What it means
Part 24	Summary judgment	The case is so clear-cut that there is no point in having a trial (Note: defendants as well as claimants can ask for summary judgment)
Part 25	Interim applications	Applications after proceedings have started but before trial; for example, injunctions and interim payments. Except for interim injunctions, does not apply to the small claims track
Part 27	Small claims track	
Part 28	Fast claims track	
Part 29	Multi track	
Part 31	Disclosure of documents	Each side must let the other side see any documents that might be relevant to the case; does not apply to the small claims track
Part 32	Evidence	Oral and written evidence or witnesses relating to the facts
Part 35	Expert evidence	The rules governing expert reports, meetings of experts, questions to experts, etc.
Part 36	Offers of settlement	How to make a formal offer of settlement; does not apply to the small claims track
Parts 44 and 48	Costs	What the court will take into account when deciding what costs order should be made
Part 52	Appeals	How to conduct an appeal and what the court will take into account

Glossary

Action: Claim going through the court.

Advocate: Lawyer (either solicitor or barrister) who presents a case in court.

Affidavit: A sworn witness statement.

Affirm: A solemn undertaking that the evidence a witness is giving is true.

After the event (ATE): A policy taken out after the event leading to the claim, which insures against the risk of losing the claim and having to pay the other side's costs.

Allocation questionnaire: Form completed by both parties after a defence has been filed.

Allow (an appeal): To agree the appeal should succeed.

Alternative Dispute Resolution (ADR): Alternatives to court action for resolving civil disputes.

Appeal: Asking a higher court to reverse or vary a judge's decision.

Appellant: Party making the appeal.

Applicant: Party who makes an application.

Application: Formal request to the court.

Arbitration: Formal method of deciding a claim without going to court, common in building and other commercial disputes.

Attachment of earnings: Order for deductions to be made from the earnings of a judgment debtor to pay money owing under the judgment.

Balance of convenience: See *balance of justice*.

Balance of justice: Balancing the claimant's need for immediate protection against the defendant's right to a fair trial on an interim application.

Balance of probabilities: More likely than not (civil standard of proof).

Barrister: Lawyer specialising in advice and advocacy.

Before the event (BTE): A legal expenses insurance policy that was in place before the event leading to the claim.

Beyond reasonable doubt: So that you are sure (the criminal standard of proof).

Breach: Disobey, flout.

Burden of proof: Having to prove your case (usually the claimant).

Case management: The way in which the court controls the progress of the claim up to trial.

Case management conference (CMC): Court hearing attended by all parties to sort out directions and get the claim to trial.

Charging order: Order that allows property or other assets to be sold to pay money owing under a judgment debt.

Circuit judge: County Court judge who deals with fast track and multi track trials, appeals from the district judge and interim applications in more complicated cases.

Civil Procedure Rules (CPR): Rules governing how claims are processed in the civil courts.

Claim form: The court form you or your solicitor need to complete to start the claim.

Claimant: Party bringing the claim.

Claims farmer: Company or firm which canvasses for civil claims.

Claims manager: Company dealing with accident and negligence claims on a 'no win no fee' basis.

Committal: Send to prison.

Community Legal Services (CLS): An offshoot of the government department responsible for making legal advice and representation available at little or no cost – mostly through legal aid.

Conditional fee agreement (CFA): Arrangement whereby lawyers act for a client on a 'no win no fee' basis.

Conference: Private meeting with your barrister, solicitor and, possibly, expert witness(es).

Consent order: An order made by the court that everyone agrees to.

Consultation: The same as a conference but presided over by a QC.

Contemnor: Person who has disobeyed the court.

Contempt of court: Do something forbidden by the court.

Contingency fee: Arrangement where part of any damages awarded is used to pay legal costs.

Costs order: Order determining who should pay the legal costs.

Counsel: See *barrister*.

Counterclaim: Defendant's claim against the claimant.

Cross undertakings: Where each party promises the other not to act unlawfully.

Cross-examination: Critical questioning conducted by the lawyer for the opposing party.

Damages: Financial compensation.

Declaration: Statement by the court of the legal position.

Defence: Defendant's statement of case.

Defendant: Party against whom the claim is brought.

Deputy High Court judge: A lawyer who sits as a High Court judge for a few weeks every year.

Detailed assessment of costs: Where a district judge decides the amount the party paying costs must pay after the end of the case.

Directions: Orders made by the court for the things that need to be done to get the claim ready for trial.

Disallow costs: To refuse to make an order that the other party should pay the amount and/or the costs claimed.

Disbursement: Extra expenses over and above the solicitor's fees.

Discharge (an order): Cancel.

Disclosure: Process of giving the other party access to any documents that are relevant to the claim.

Disposal hearing: Short hearing to decide the amount of damages to be awarded where a judgment in default has been entered.

District judge: County Court judge who deals with interim applications and small claims and fast track trials.

Draft order: Terms of an order prepared by one or both parties in the hope that the court will approve it.

Drop hands agreement: Where the parties agree to walk away from the claim and each pay their own costs.

Enforcement: Ensuring that a judgment is complied with.

Examination in chief: Questions put by a party's own lawyer.

Exhibit: A document or photograph that forms part of the evidence of a witness and is attached to their statement.

Expert: An independent witness who has particular expertise in an area or profession relevant to the claim.

Fast track: Procedure for dealing with straightforward claims worth between £5,000 and £10,000.

To file or lodge a document: To send or give it to the court.

Freezing order: An order that stops someone disposing of their assets.

Hearsay evidence: Secondhand account of events or conversations.

Indemnity costs: Costs assessed on the basis that the benefit of any doubt about what is fair should be given to the person receiving them.

Inspection: Making the documents on the disclosure list that are not privileged available to the other party.

Institute of Legal Executives (ILEX): The body responsible for training and regulating legal executives.

Instruct: Employ a lawyer or expert to act for you.

Interim: Between the issue of proceedings and trial.

Interim payment: Payment made before trial on account of damages which the court is likely to award.

Issue: (proceedings or an application) To start in the court.

Joint expert: An expert working for both parties.

Judgment creditor: Person who is owed money under a judgment or costs order.

Judgment debtor: Person who owes money under a judgment or costs order.

Judgment in default: Judgment given because the defendant has not filed the acknowledgement of service or a defence.

Leading question: Question that is phrased in such a way that it invites a particular reply.

Legal executive: Someone who has experience of legal work and/or qualifications obtained through the Institute of Legal Executives (ILEX). Some legal executives go on to qualify as solicitors.

Letter of claim: A letter that puts the defendant on notice that the claimant intends to take court action.

Liability: Legal responsibility.

Limitation period: Time allowed for bringing a claim.

Listing a case or application: Setting the date for the hearing.

Lists: Listing all the documents in the possession or control of a party (whether or not they are privileged).

Litigant in person: Party who is not legally represented.

Litigant/party: Person bringing or defending a claim.

Litigation friend: Someone bringing a claim either on behalf of a child or an adult who lacks the mental capacity to understand the proceedings.

Master: Specialist judge dealing with High Court interim applications and costs at the Royal Courts of Justice in London.

Mediation: Using a neutral third party to negotiate a settlement.

Multi track: Procedure for dealing with more complex or valuable claims.

Non-party disclosure: Disclosure of documents held by someone who is not a party to the claim.

Ombudsman: Body appointed to investigate complaints about services.

Overriding objective: The principle that all civil claims should be dealt with quickly and fairly.

Paginated: Numbered pages.

Paralegal: Someone who does not have a legal qualification but who has some experience in legal work and may be employed to deal with civil claims.

Particulars of claim: Claimant's statement of case.

Personal service: Arranging for documents to be handed over personally to the party concerned.

Pleadings: See *statement of case.*

Power of arrest: Where the police can arrest someone for breaching a court order.

Pre-action disclosure: Disclosure before proceedings have started.

Pre-action protocol: Procedure for initiating a civil claim.

Pre-trial checklist: Checklist completed by each party to enable the court to list the claim for trial.

Pre-trial review: Similar to a CMC but specifically for more complicated cases to make sure everything is ready for trial.

Privilege: Protection from disclosure.

Procedural: Relating to steps that need to be taken to get the case ready for trial.

Proceedings: Taking a claim through the court.

Queens Counsel (QC): Senior barrister.

Recorder: Lawyer who sits as a part-time judge in the County Court.

Re-examination: Questions put by a party's own barrister to clarify points raised in cross-examination.

Remedy: Action ordered by the court to try to make amends.

Reply: Document in which the claimant specifically responds to the defence. Only really necessary in very complicated cases or where the defence raises a completely new argument.

Respondent: Party on the receiving end of an application or appeal.

Return date: Date set by the court for a full hearing of an application.

Rights of audience: The right to speak at a court hearing.

Risks of litigation: The risk that even in a very strong case something might go wrong.

Search order: An order allowing premises to be searched for specified types of evidence.

Security for costs: Payment into court of a sum of money by the claimant that provide the defendant with some security if the claimant loses.

Service/serve: Ensuring that the formal court papers are received by other parties to the claim.

Set aside (an order): Cancel so that to all intents and purposes it was never made.

Skeleton argument: Written argument prepared by each party in support of their case.

Small claims track: Procedure for dealing with low value claims.

Solicitor: A fully qualified and trained lawyer whose professional work is regulated by the Law Society who deals with the day-to-day conduct of the claim.

Specific disclosure: Disclosure of specified documents.

Standard costs: Costs assessed on the basis that the benefit of any doubt about what is fair should be given to the paying party.

Standard disclosure: Disclosing the documents that are relevant to the case and not privileged.

Standard of proof: The level of proof required to win a claim.

Statement of case: Document in a party to a civil claim sets out their case.

Stay of execution: Order preventing successful party from enforcing a judgment or costs order.

Stay in proceedings: Putting the claim on hold – usually to allow settlement negotiations to take place.

Strike out: When either the claimant or defendant is not allowed to pursue their claim any further.

Success fee: Percentage increase on a lawyer's fee paid under a conditional fee agreement if the case is won.

Summary assessment of costs: Where the amount of costs to be paid is decided at the hearing.

Summary judgment: Judgment entered before trial because the case is so clear-cut.

Third party: A party who the defendant blames for the damage suffered by the claimant.

Third party debt order: Order for a bank or building society to pay money held in a judgment debtor's account to a judgment creditor.

Tomlin Order: A type of order that allows the parties to settle the claim without judgment being entered.

Trainee solicitor: Someone who has passed all the solicitors' exams and is now working under supervision under a two-year training contract to become fully qualified.

Trial bundle: Paginated files of documents for everyone to use at the trial.

Trial window: Period of time specified by the court when the trial will be listed.

Undertaking in damages: Claimant's promise to make good any financial loss the defendant may suffer if an interim injunction is made.

Waive: Give up/relinquish.

Walking possession: Agreement that certain items belonging to the judgment debtor will remain in his possession but can be seized and sold if necessary to pay the judgment.

Warrant of execution: County Court order that allows bailiffs to seize goods for sale to enforce a judgment.

Without notice: Not telling the respondent to an application about it before the first hearing takes place.

Without prejudice: Making a concession or offer of settlement, which the trial judge will not know about if the claim goes to trial.

Witness summons: Court order for a witness to attend court.

Writ of fi fa: High Court order that allows enforcement officer to seize goods for sale to enforce a judgment.

Useful addresses

Acas
See the website for regional office addresses
Helpline: 08457 47 47 47
(Monday–Friday, 8am–6pm)
www.acas.org.uk

ADRnow
(Alternative disputes resolution)
Advice Services Alliance
12th Floor, New London Bridge House
25 London Bridge Street
London SE1 9SG
www.adrnow.org.uk

The Association of Law Costs Draftsmen
47 Church St
Great Baddow
Chelmsford, CM2 7JA
Tel: 01379 741404
www.alcd.org.uk

Bar Council
289–293 High Holborn
London WC1V 7HZ
Tel: 020 7242 0082
www.barcouncil.org.uk

Bar Pro Bono Unit
289–293 High Holborn
London WC1V 7HZ
Tel: 020 7611 9500
www.barprobono.org.uk

Citizens Advice Bureau
Look in your local phone book or go to
www.adviceguide.org.uk

Community Legal Service
Tel: 0845 345 4345
www.clsdirect.org.uk

Consumer Credit Counselling Service
Wade House
Merrion Centre
Leeds LS2 8NG
Helpline: 0800 138 1111
(Monday–Friday, 8am–8pm)
www.cccs.co.uk

Criminal Injuries Compensation Authority
Tay House
300 Bath Street
Glasgow G2 4LN
Tel: 0141 331 2726
Helpline: 0800 358 3601
(Monday–Friday, 9am–8pm; Saturday, 10am–6pm)
www.cica.co.uk

Financial Ombudsman Service
The Financial Ombudsman Service
South Quay Plaza
183 Marsh Wall
London E14 9SR
Helpline: 0845 080 1800
www.financial-ombudsman.org.uk

Her Majesty's Court Service
Customer Service Unit
5th Floor
Clive House
Petty France
London SW1H 9EX
Customer help desk: 0845 601 5935
(Monday–Friday, 9am–5pm)
www.hmcourts-service.gov.uk

High Court Enforcement Officers
Association
PO Box 180
Winsford CW7 2WP
www.hceoa.org.uk

Housing Ombudsman Service
81 Aldwych
London WC2B 4HN
Tel: 020 7421 3800
www.ihos.org.uk

Law Society of England and Wales
113 Chancery Lane
London WC2A 1PL
Tel: 020 7242 1222
www.lawsociety.org.uk

Law Society of Ireland
Blackhall Place
Dublin 7
Ireland
Tel: 03531 672 4800
www.lawsociety.ie

Law Society of Northern Ireland
Law Society House
98 Victoria Street
Belfast BT1 3JZ
Northern Ireland
Tel: 028 90 231614
www.lawsoc-ni.org

Law Society of Scotland
26 Drumsheugh Gardens
Edinburgh EH3 7YR
Tel: 0131 226 7411
www.lawscot.org.uk

Law Works
10–13 Lovat Lane
London, EC3R 8DN
Tel: 020 7929 5601
www.lawworks.org.uk

Legal Services Ombudsman
3rd Floor
Sunlight House
Quay Street
Manchester
Tel: 0845 601 0794
www.olso.org

Local Government Ombudsman

(London boroughs North of the River Thames
(including Richmond but not including Harrow or
Tower Hamlets), Essex, Kent, Surrey, Suffolk, East
and West Sussex, Berkshire, Buckinghamshire,
Hertfordshire and the City of Coventry)

Local Government Ombudsman
10th Floor
Millbank Tower
Millbank
London SW1P 4QP
Tel: 020 7217 4620
www.lgo.org.uk

(London borough of Tower Hamlets, City of
Birmingham, Solihull MBC, Cheshire, Derbyshire,
Nottinghamshire, Lincolnshire, Warwickshire and
the North of England (except the cities of
Lancaster, Manchester and York)

Local Government Ombudsman
Beverley House
17 Shipton Road
York YO30 5FZ
Tel: 01904 380200
www.lgo.org.uk

(London boroughs south of the River Thames
(except Richmond) and Harrow; the cities of
Lancaster, Manchester and York; and the rest of
England, not included in the areas above)

Local Government Ombudsman
The Oaks
No 2 Westwood Way
Westwood Business Park
Coventry CV4 8JB
Tel: 024 7682 0000
www.lgo.org.uk

Ministry of Justice
Selborne House
54 Victoria Street
London SW1E 6QW
Tel: 020 7210 8500
www.justice.gov.uk

National Debtline
Tricorn House
51–53 Hagley Road
Edgbaston
Birmingham B16 8TP
Tel: 0808 808 4000 (Monday–Friday,
9am–9pm; Saturday 9.30am –1pm).
Please leave a message to request an
information pack or factsheet.

National Disability Conciliation Service
St Lawrence House
Broad Street
Bristol BS1 2HF
Tel: 0117 914 2380
www.dcs-gb.net

Ombudsman for Estate Agents
Beckett House
4 Bridge Street
Salisbury
Wiltshire SP1 2LX
Tel: 01722 333306
www.oea.co.uk

The Parliamentary and Health Service
Ombudsman
Millbank Tower
Millbank
London SW1P 4QP
Helpline 0845 015 4033
www.ombudsman.org.uk

Pensions Ombudsman
11 Belgrave Road
London SW1V 1RB
Tel: 020 7834 9144
www.pensions-ombudsman.org.uk

The Registry Trust
173–175 Cleveland Street
London W1T 6QR
Tel: 020 7380 0133 (Monday–Friday,
10am–4pm)
www.registry-trust.org.uk

Solicitors Regulation Authority
Ipsley Court
Berrington Close
Redditch B98 0TD
Tel: 0870 606 2555 (Monday–Friday,
9am–5pm)
www.sra.org.uk

Which? Legal Service
Tel: 0800 252 100
www.whichlegalservice.co.uk

Further reading

PRACTITIONERS' BOOKS

These are the standard text books that lawyers use when preparing or advising on a case. They are very expensive, but most reference libraries should have copies of them.

Chitty on Contracts 2 volumes (Sweet & Maxwell, London, 2006) (covers all types of contract and contractual situation, including employment, sale of goods, etc.)

Clerk & Lindsell on Torts (Sweet & Maxwell, London, 2006)) (covers cases involving negligence (accidents, professional negligence, etc.), nuisance (where the acts of a neighbour affect enjoyment of your property, e.g. by causing physical damage or other disturbance, such as noise and libel)

Green Book, Civil Court Practice, published annually in 2 volumes (Butterworths, London 2006)

White Book, Civil Procedure, published annually in 2 volumes (Sweet & Maxwell, London, 2007)

OTHER USEFUL REFERENCE BOOKS

These specialist books are written for lawyers and cover specific types of civil claim:

Boundaries, Walls & Fences, Trevor Aldridge (Oyez)

Employer's Liability at Common Law, John Munkman (Butterworths, London, 2006)

Holiday Law, David Grant and Stephen Mason (Sweet & Maxwell, London, 2007)

Injunctions, David Bean (Sweet & Maxwell, London, 2006)

Inheritance Act Claims, Law and Practice, Sidney Ross (Sweet & Maxwell, London, 2001)

Personal Injury Handbook, Nicholas Waller (The Law Society, London, 2005)

Repairs, Tenants' Rights, Luba & Knafler (Legal Action Group, London, 1999)

Residential Possession Proceedings, Gary Webber and Daniel Dover (Sweet & Maxwell, London, 2005)

Sale of Goods & Consumer Credit, Paul Dobson (Sweet & Maxwell, London, 2000)

Travel Law & Litigation, Alan Saggerson (XPL Publishing, St Albans, 2004)

For a cheaper and more user-friendly approach to the law:

Contract Law Directions, Richard and Damian Taylor (OUP, Oxford 2007)

Consumer Law (Key Facts Law), Jacqueline Martin and Chris Turner (Hodder Arnold, London, 2005)

Tort Law (Key Facts Law), Chris Turner (Hodder Arnold, London, 2001) (covers negligence, nuisance, animals, civil liberties, assault to the person and defamation)

Index

215

Which? Legal Service

Sorting out any kind of dispute can be a real headache. Thankfully, Which? Legal Service has seen it all before and knows how to get you justice. Whatever your problem, a team of qualified, experienced lawyers are available on the end of the phone to help solve it.

The Which? Legal Service provides three months' unlimited telephone legal advice from top consumer lawyers for just £12.75 per quarter. Which? and Which? online subscribers receive a discount of £3 per quarter so pay just £9.75 and, because the service is from Which?, there are no hidden fees or extras. Just independent expert advice you can trust.

Call or visit the website to get a quick resolution to your problem
0800 252 100
www.whichlegalservice.co.uk

Which? lawyers can advise you directly on a wide range of problems involving:
- consumer law
- employment law
- holiday problems
- neighbour disputes
- parking, speeding and clamping fines
- probate administration
- small business contract disputes (partnership and sole traders only) where the business has acted as a consumer

Which? Books

Other books in this series

Working For Yourself
Mike Pywell and Bill Hilton
ISBN: 978 1 84490 040 4
Price £10.99

Working for Yourself is a practical and straightforward guide, aimed at people who are planning the jump from a salaried, permanent contract to a freelance/entrepreneurial lifestyle. Pointing out the benefits and prospective pitfalls of being self-employed, this essential guide then details pertinent financial and legal information, as well as suggesting when and where to seek professional help.

Managing Your Debt
Phillip Inman
ISBN: 978 1 84490 041 1
Price £10.99

Managing your Debt is a practical and straightforward guide to managing your finances and getting your money, and your life, back on track. It covers a wide range of topics including how to identify and deal with priority debts, the best way to make a debt management plan, who to write to and what to say and what to expect should you ever face bankruptcy or an individual voluntary agreement.

Develop Your Property
Kate Faulkner
ISBN: 978 1 84490 038 1
Price £10.99

Develop your Property is aimed at the thousands of people in the UK who are looking to make a serious and long-term investment in their property. Covering planning permission and building regulations, this guide deals with property development in a jargon-free and unbiased manner.

Which? Books

Other books in this series

Divorce and Splitting Up
Imogen Clout
ISBN: 978 1 84490 034 3
Price £10.99

Divorce, separation, dissolution of a civil partnership or simply splitting up with a partner is never easy – the emotional upheaval, legal complexities and financial implications make even the most amicable parting a demanding business; when children are involved, couples are in dispute and property needs to be divided the whole process can be fraught with difficulties. *Divorce and Splitting Up* offers comprehensive, clear, step-by-step guidance through the whole process, explaining how the law works, drawing attention to key considerations and looking at ways of minimising unnecessary conflict and costs.

Giving and Inheriting
Jonquil Lowe
ISBN: 978 1 84490 032 9
Price £10.99

Inheritance tax (IHT) is becoming a major worry for more and more people. Rising house prices have pushed up the value of typical estates to a level where they are liable to be taxed at 40% on everything over £285,000. *Giving and Inheriting* is an essential guide to estate planning and tax liability, offering up-to-the–minute advice from an acknowledged financial expert, this book will help people reduce the tax bill faced by their heirs and allow many to avoid IHT altogether.

The Tax Handbook 2007/8
Tony Levene
ISBN: 978 1 84490 039 8
Price £10.99

Make sense of the complicated rules, legislation and red-tape with the *Tax Handbook 2007/8*. Written by Guardian finance journalist and tax expert Tony Levene, this essential guide gives expert advice on all aspects of the UK tax system and does the footwork for you. It includes information on finding the right accountant and how to get the best from them, advice on NI contributions, tax credits for families and the self-assessment form. An indispensable guide for anyone who pays tax.

Which? Books

Which? Books provide impartial, expert advice on everyday matters from finance to law, property to major life events. We also publish the country's most trusted restaurant guide, *The Which? Good Food Guide*. To find out more about Which? Books, log on to www.which.co.uk or call 01903 828557.

❝ Which? tackles the issues that really matter to consumers and gives you the advice and active support you need to buy the right products. **❞**